Collecting Activism, Archi Wall Street

I0046628

Collecting Activism, Archiving Occupy Wall Street explores the material collections produced by participants of Occupy Wall Street in 2011 that bear witness to the experience and agency of 'the 99%'.

Examining processes of collection development as a lens through which to investigate the sociology of protest and reform movements, the book questions what contribution a dual study of the material culture of dissent and the production of a collection hosting the material culture of dissent might offer to a range of disciplines and practices. It asks if and how a collections-based study can test the propositions, tactics, and limits of activism from archival, museological, and political perspectives.

Collecting Activism, Archiving Occupy Wall Street draws from interdisciplinary fields, including museum studies, collection studies, archive studies, cultural studies, and public history. It will be a valuable resource for scholars and practitioners engaged with contemporary cause-based collecting, activist archiving, public history, and the cultural politics and sociology of social reform movements. It models strategies for 'activating' historical archives and collections-based data, and for engaging with autoethnographic records to represent and analyze the material residue of protest and reform movements today.

Kylie Message is Professor of Public Humanities in the Humanities Research Centre and Associate Dean (Research) for the College of Arts and Social Sciences at the Australian National University. Her recent publications include *The Disobedient Museum: Writing at the Edge*, *Museums and Racism*, and *Museums and Social Activism: Engaged Protest*. She is the Founding Series Editor of 'Museums in Focus'.

Museums in Focus
Series Editor: Kylie Message, Australian National University, Australia

Committed to the articulation of big, even risky ideas, in small format publications, 'Museums in Focus' challenges authors and readers to experiment with, innovate, and press museums and the intellectual frameworks through which we view these. It offers a platform for approaches that radically rethink the relationships between cultural and intellectual dissent and crisis and debates about museums, politics, and the broader public sphere.

'Museums in Focus' is motivated by the intellectual hypothesis that museums are not innately 'useful', 'safe', or even 'public' places, and that recalibrating our thinking about them might benefit from adopting a more radical and oppositional form of logic and approach. Examining this problem requires a level of comfort with (or at least tolerance of) the idea of crisis, dissent, protest, and radical thinking, and authors might benefit from considering how cultural and intellectual crisis, regeneration, and anxiety have been dealt with in other disciplines and contexts.

Recently published titles

Collecting Activism, Archiving Occupy Wall Street
Kylie Message

Museums, Infinity and the Culture of Protocols
Ethnographic Collections and Source Communities
Howard Morphy

https://www.routledge.com/Museums-in-Focus/book-series/MIF

MUSEUMS IN FOCUS

Logo by James Verdon (2017)

Collecting Activism, Archiving Occupy Wall Street

Kylie Message

Routledge
Taylor & Francis Group

LONDON AND NEW YORK

First published 2020
by Routledge
2 Park Square, Milton Park, Abingdon, Oxon OX14 4RN

and by Routledge
605 Third Avenue, New York, NY 10017

First issued in paperback 2021

Routledge is an imprint of the Taylor & Francis Group, an informa business

© 2020 Kylie Message

The right of Kylie Message to be identified as author of this work has been asserted by her in accordance with sections 77 and 78 of the Copyright, Designs and Patents Act 1988.

All rights reserved. No part of this book may be reprinted or reproduced or utilised in any form or by any electronic, mechanical, or other means, now known or hereafter invented, including photocopying and recording, or in any information storage or retrieval system, without permission in writing from the publishers.

Trademark notice: Product or corporate names may be trademarks or registered trademarks, and are used only for identification and explanation without intent to infringe.

British Library Cataloguing-in-Publication Data
A catalogue record for this book is available from the British Library

Library of Congress Cataloging-in-Publication Data
Names: Message, Kylie, author.
Title: Collecting activism, archiving occupy / Kylie Message.
Description: New York: Routledge, 2019. | Series: Museums in focus |
Includes bibliographical references and index.
Identifiers: LCCN 2019027843 (print) | LCCN 2019027844 (ebook)
| ISBN 9781138240124 (hardback) | ISBN 9781315294094 (ebook) |
ISBN 9781315294087 (adobe pdf) | ISBN 9781315294063 (mobi) |
ISBN 9781315294070 (epub)
Subjects: LCSH: Occupy Wall Street (Movement)–Archives. | Occupy
movement–New York (State)–New York–Records and correspondence. |
Protest movements–United States–History–21st century–Records and
correspondence. | Equality–United States. | Income distribution–
United States.
Classification: LCC HC110.I5 M43 2019 (print) | LCC HC110.I5 (ebook) |
DDC 026/.32244097471–dc23
LC record available at https://lccn.loc.gov/2019027843
LC ebook record available at https://lccn.loc.gov/2019027844

ISBN 13: 978-0-367-77781-4 (pbk)
ISBN 13: 978-1-138-24012-4 (hbk)

Typeset in Times
by Deanta Global Publishing Services, Chennai, India

Anonymous graffiti, Athens. Image and logo by James Verdon (2017).

For Oscar

Contents

Figures

Acknowledgments

The research for this book has been complex and has taken several years. While this is not unusual, it does go some way to explaining why it came to be known as the 'impossible project'. My main debt of gratitude goes to Amy Roberts. It is because of her and other members of the Occupy Archives Working Group that the collection has a future. Although this book will come up short in representing their visionary and significant work, I hope it builds awareness of the intellectual and practical contributions they made to activist archiving. My approach was influenced by a chapter written by Sian Evans, Anna Perricci, and Amy Roberts ("'Why Archive?" And Other Important Questions Asked by Occupiers', in M. Morrone (ed.), 2014, *Informed Agitation: Library and Information Skills in Social Justice Movements and Beyond*, Sacramento, CA: Library Juice Press), which offers insight and reflection into the process of archiving Occupy. I acknowledge Timothy Johnson, and very warmly thank the archivists and interns at Tamiment Library. I am also grateful to those at the Smithsonian Institution, the Museum of the City of New York, and the Interference Archive in Brooklyn for their discussions and for opening collections for me.

I am grateful for research funding and time provided by the Research School of Humanities at the Arts, and the College of Arts and Social Sciences at the Australian National University. I thank the College of Arts and Humanities Institute (CAHI) at Indiana University, Bloomington, for hosting me throughout the summer of 2018. I continue to be indebted to Heidi Lowther, my exceptional editor at Routledge.

My colleagues at ANU have provided a generosity of spirit and intellectual stimulation, patience, friendship, and perhaps most importantly, a lot of laughter: Penny Brew, Ann Evans, Katrina Grant, Terhi Nurmikko-Fuller, Paul Pickering. Kate Bowan and Anna Edmundson also provided astute and critical feedback on a near-final draft that led to a substantive and significant restructuring of the manuscript. Many brilliant students have x *Acknowledgments*

provided a source of inspiration and instruction, particularly Mia Thornton and Eleanor Foster, and I acknowledge Anna Edmundson's 2013 ANU PhD dissertation, 'For Science, Salvage, and State: Official Collecting in Colonial New Guinea', which considered innovative new ways to approach ethnographic collections analysis and informed the approach I employed in this book. I also acknowledge the invaluable ongoing impact of Howard Morphy's remarkable models of embedded practice for undertaking collections-based research, and Maya Haviland's timely tearoom reminder to 'just tell the story'.

Finally, I acknowledge my rebel muse, Oscar Johnston. I thank my partner in life, Guy Jones; and Ezra Johnston and Jill and Bob Message. Expressing adequate gratitude to my family is difficult, an almost impossible project in its own right.

Go document history as it happens[1]

In the summer of 2018 I met with Amy Roberts at Zuccotti Park, a three-quarter-acre privately owned public park in Lower Manhattan. It had been the initial venue for the Occupy Wall Street movement, and Roberts had been one of the principal instigators of the movement's Archives Working Group. It felt urgent but impossible, the way Roberts talked about the collection created by the Archives Working Group. She wanted me to know how important it was for American political and economic history, for 'the people', what it meant for the Occupy Wall Street movement, and what it meant for her personally.

Roberts and I had been in contact for a while, from the final phases of Obama's administration in 2016 into the first months of Trump's presidency the following year. It was coming up to seven years since Zuccotti Park/Wall Street had been occupied (from September 17 to November 15, 2011).[2] Today there is almost no remaining evidence of the occupation. The power outlets are still gaffer-taped over, but now people are allowed to sleep and lounge on the benches during the day. Unlike most other tiny parks in the area, there are no 'This is a private space' plaques on the ground. I was pleased to find one remaining sign of resistance – a 'Re-occupy' engraving in the concrete pavement at the base of the traffic lights at the Cedar and Trinity construction site, down a bit from a line of pizza places. Roberts hadn't previously seen it.[3]

I wondered what I was even looking for in returning to the site with Roberts. Some kind of left-over material residue or proof of evidence linking the collections with this place? Perhaps there would be an official-looking commemorative sign or symbol acknowledging the part that Liberty Plaza had played in establishing Occupy Wall Street as a movement that fought to progress American aspirations of political, cultural, and economic equality and freedom (Manski 2011; Schneider n.d.). But then again, who would pay for that? Brookfields Corporation had already made its position clear by naming the site's post 9/11 reconstruction in honor of the company's US chairman, John E. Zuccotti, and by reinstituting the statue of a bronze

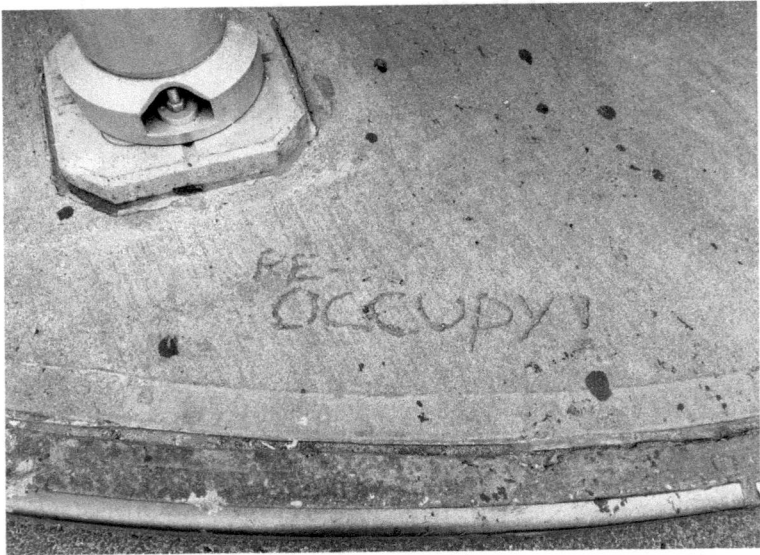

Figure 0.1 Graffiti in pavement, corner of Cedar and Trinity Streets, New York, NY.
Photograph by Kylie Message.

businessman sitting on a bench (*Double Check*, 1982, by John Seward Johnson II; Brookfield Properties 2006; Dunlap 2006).

The City of New York continues to have an uneasy relationship with the Occupy Wall Street movement. Zuccotti Park, a concrete plaza, is a block uptown from the September 11 Memorial, a block away from the US Stock Exchange, and about ten minutes diagonally south of Foley Square. The nineteenth-century fashion for heroic bronze monuments of state heroes, largely replaced by the abstract expressionism commissioned by corporations and regional councils to signal post-war confidence in the country's democratic institutions and economy, has given way to more ephemeral icons, assertions, and commemorations of acute actions as well as enduring political process. The shift is exemplified by the literal face-off between two statues, *Charging Bull* (by Arturo Di Modica, 1989) and *Fearless Girl* (by Kristen Visbal, 2017), which share the intersection of Broadway and Whitehall Streets. Transformations in the iconography of protest have also occurred in intervening years. The symbolic impact of the 'V for Vendetta' Guy Fawkes-style masks worn by anti-establishment groups (like the hacker group, Anonymous) during Occupy Wall Street have been surpassed as a signifier of participatory political process and changing awareness about movements for equality by the pink knitted 'Pussyhats' worn at Women's Marches. The idea of the 99%, which was central to the protest, has if anything expanded.

As the material culture products of protest have diversified since Occupy Wall Street, the interest of museums in the events they represent has escalated, and swift efforts to collect items as evidence of a changing national psyche can be observed. Even the most cursory literature review shows the mounting interest by public history and museum studies scholars in cause-based collecting and curatorial activism around events like the Women's Marches from 2017, the #MeToo movement, LGBTIQ+ rights movements, abortion (and 'right to life') activism, protest actions over race hate, youth rallies for gun control in response to high-profile school shootings in 2012 (Sandy Hook) and 2018 (Parkland, Florida), environmentalism, and indigenous rights issues including around Dakota Pipeline Access, and immigration rights (see Message 2018a for overview).

Surges in collecting activity by mainstream state and national institutions have been driven to some degree by an activist concern that social reform movements will 'only become part of political history if the images and artifacts are collected, preserved, and documented for later display and study' (Cohen-Stratyner 2017: 83).[4] This shifting concern and growing awareness about the national significance of protest and reform movements has had an impact on the public's view of collections, with American curator Barbara Cohen-Stratyner (2017: 87) suggesting that since the election of US President Donald Trump, the American public, many of whom participated in the Women's Marches in Washington DC and other places, have become more alert to the role that collections made from contemporary events play in the construction of memory and history as well as truth and identity. Perhaps in response to perceptions of a heightened need for authentication of truth claims, a rapid-response approach to collecting material and documentary evidence of political reform movements has become a function increasingly associated with social history institutions since 2011.[5]

The current proclivity for institutions to collect first and determine relevance second marks a shift from prior imperatives that debated relevance before collection occurred, particularly in the case of politically controversial material (Message 2014; Gardner 2016: 280). In the current climate – where barrages of tweets by President Trump stand *in lieu* of due government process (Reich 2019), and where increasing attempts by institutions to document (safeguard) political process through the acquisition of material evidence – our attention skims quickly from one shiny thing to the next, without stopping for reflection on the very recent history and practices of collecting activism that developed alongside the events they have sought to capture. As a result, the 'official' collection of public activism by and for activists continues to remain a little-known and vulnerable process today, despite the publicity that activist events, products, and outputs have attracted on national and global stages. The practice of cause-based collecting has also generated some ethical issues around ownership, representation, authority, and agency that have been overlooked in the haste to collect from ephemeral protest and reform actions, movements, and rallies.

Groundwork: The here and now

As a site, Zuccotti Park, even with the benefit of the information provided by a passing tour guide, didn't tell me much.[6] It was only after Roberts came along that I was able to refocus my goal, from reading the site as a source to engaging with it as a subject mediated through her conversation. I was reminded of the difficulty I had in understanding the semiotics of the park later, when I read Ann Laura Stoler's argument that 'scholars need to move from archive-as-source to archive-as-subject' (Stoler 2002: 87).[7] Stoler argues that scholars need to employ different disciplinary tools to engage with the form and context of materials in the repository. She says we need

Figure 0.2 Zuccotti Park signage, New York, NY.

Photograph by Kylie Message.

to identify and explore the subjectivity of the materials rather than simply mining the collection for what the information it holds *prima facie* 'says'. Her advice conveys a powerful pathway for navigating the complex life histories and diverse infrastructures circulating through and around physical cultural sites such as parks and archives. It encourages a focused study of the context (Zuccotti Park) for material artifact creation, use, and collection.

Like many public spaces, Zuccotti Park exists as an in-between or contested zone, a space that cannot be adequately accounted for or contained by singular descriptions. It hosts distracted, routine, and tactical pedestrian shortcuts and extended lunch breaks, as well as a multitude of diverse economic and social transactions and interactions. Disobedient spaces like these have long been used for occupations, encampments, and social reform protest events, and have attracted a multitude of nomenclature in museological and other literature (see Message 2018a for overview). These spaces are consistent, for example, with the contact zone trope popularized by James Clifford (1997), and with what collections scholar Susan Pearce has called shadowlands. 'Collecting as a process works in the shadowland', she explains, 'by making its meaning on the edge where the practices of the past, the politics of present power, and the poetic capacity of each human being blur together' (Pearce 1998: 1). They offer physical but often unmarked archives of human action.

The pathways presented by Stoler and Pearce for reading collections as places for research and questioning resonate with the invocation by American studies scholar, Kandice Chuh, for researchers to think expansively and relationally about the current day, the 'here and now'. 'Let's start here', says Chuh, explaining that for her, '"America" is not the object of American Studies. It's actually a space through which we think … to ask questions that we couldn't otherwise ask, or address questions that we couldn't otherwise address' (Chuh quoted in Mesle 2017). Rather than generating a 'museums are good to think' typology,[8] this approach encourages a shift from identifying America as an end-point or source (which implies the kind of unchanging paradigm shared also by stereotypes of archives as dusty and unchanging, inaccessible and tomb-like) to unpicking the concept of America so that it becomes a place from which to *commence* our investigations (a subject). This shift relies on recognition of 'the specificity of the here and now, and history and context', and opens up different options for examining questions about humanization, power, possibility, and nation (Chuh in Mesle 2017). *This* America sounds something like the shadowlands from which Pearce's observations about collecting take place, and has similarities with the museum-like boundary zones theorized in *The Disobedient Museum* (Message 2018a), which also provide an analogy for understanding Zuccotti Park historically and today.

Archive as subject

Despite their respective foci on institutions and on the national contexts in which institutions are often held (accountable), both Stoler's work and Chuh's interview offer insightful ways to think about archives, collections, and museums that hold and represent the histories of diverse people and populations. They counsel us, as do Pearce's frameworks for analyzing contemporary collections, to consider our sites of research not as inert or objective sources of information, but as subjective assemblages through which we can think urgent sociopolitical questions. Roberts and other members of the Occupy Wall Street Archives Working Group also recognized the pluralist importance of archives and objects. They understood the role archives hold in producing or contributing to official versions of historical memory, as well as the ability of collections to represent the physical evidence of diversity and counter-narratives.[9] Indeed, the archive was, for this group, the main instrument of resistance and the main vehicle through which they advocated for the Occupy movement.

The Occupy Wall Street Archives Working Group was one of more than a hundred working groups affiliated with Occupy Wall Street.[10] The group's remit was to 'ensure that the OWS will own its past. Its mission is to keep OWS historically self-conscious, and guarantee that our history will be accessible to the public' (Roberts 2011a). Their emphasis on the tools of archival work and on collecting the material residue of contemporary protest from the site put them at odds with the consensus opinions voiced at Occupy General Assemblies. Yet they did not see their aim to contribute to the institutional historical record as necessarily antithetical to the independence of the collection or the political cause represented by the movement. Rather, in the spirit of what I have elsewhere called the disobedient museology (Message 2018a), working group members saw their collections – 'what you have' (see Roberts n.d.h: 15) – as offering a fuller representation of 'the situation' of contemporary life, and as providing a picture of the challenges of archiving social movements (see Roberts n.d.h:15).[11]

The group was clear in voicing its shared view that archives have a unique ability to represent the materials as well as the situation of creation, use, and collection of protest and reform movements. Their outlook was consistent with arguments by Stoler (2002), and Chuh (in Mesle 2017). One member of the working group explained:

> Because taking over the park was a specific direct action, like it was a specific event and a specific time, and whatever that came out of that time can't be duplicated … [T]he objects [alone] carry those memories. And everybody sees those objects with different attachments.

The object stays when the actual event is over. And you can help piece together a timeline and understand things in a different way when you have an archive. ... it gives you access to something that you weren't part of. And being part of it, you still have access to it because there's parts of Occupy that I wasn't a part of and when I see the project, I'm like, 'Oh yeah, that's amazing!' It gives a sense of importance to the event.

(See Roberts n.d.h: 10)

These comments demonstrate Stoler's argument that archives – contemporary activist archives as well as colonial archives – exist as instruments of governance that can also and simultaneously create a space of possibility, which, in the case of the Occupy Archive, aimed to lead directly to the development and implementation of a new socio-economic order.

The working group sought, in other words, to appropriate and re-use the tools of their trade to create an archive that was credible (to the movement), legitimate (to professional archiving practice) *and also* disobedient (in its subversion of the dominant assumptions inherent to both). Their anti-institutional archives cannot, as such, be understood simply as 'accounts of actions or records of what people thought happened. They are records of uncertainty and doubt in how people imagined they could and might make the rubrics of rule correspond to a changing imperial world' (Stoler 2010: 4). They are also evidence of a commitment to process as a fundamental expression of democracy, which is, according to Robert Reich (2019), 'about means, not ends'. If we all agreed on the ends, Reich says, 'there'd be no need for democracy. ... But of course we don't agree, which is why the means by which we resolve our differences are so important. Those means include a constitution, a system of government based on the rule of law, and an independent judiciary', as well as historical and contemporary record-keeping instruments, organizations, and institutions. It follows then, that where I talk about anti-institutional archives, I do not infer a spirit of opposition and overthrow, but a process of appropriation, where the strategies of mainstream archiving are repurposed for the activist interests of the group.[12] I have retained the word 'institutional' here, both as a provocation and to indicate the group's work as itself being affiliated with the kind of boundary work that arises from being insider-outsiders (or outsider-insiders).

An insider-outsider approach

Uncertainty about process and a commitment to change are fundamental properties of the materials included within the collections produced by the Archives Working Group, including the records documenting their own actions. A further characteristic is debate over the narratives, both about the Occupy movement and about the Archives Working Group itself as a producer of that narrative. The self-documentation part of the archive reveals how and why certain narratives were circulated and contested or accepted. It also reiterates the importance of understanding the relationship between archives and subjectivity, including the ways in which power dynamics within groups can influence the form and contents of collections (regardless of their organizational model). This is consistent with Stoler's suggestion that:

> Whether documents are trustworthy, authentic, and reliable remain pressing questions, but a turn to the social and political conditions that produced those documents, what Carlo Ginzburg has called their 'evidentiary paradigms,' has altered the sense of what trust and reliability might signal and politically entail. The task is less to distinguish fiction from fact than to track the production and consumption of those 'facts' themselves.
>
> (Stoler 2002: 91)

The processes of acquisition and assemblage are represented in this passage as being more meaningful than the 'facts' that typically are determined via traditional attributions of financial value and historical significance. Members of the Archives Working Group believed that their participant-directed collection activity contributed directly to the larger democratic project's attention to the 'means' admired also by Reich (2019). This book's approach to writing about the archive has been informed by these process-oriented approaches. When I say 'let's start here', what I really mean is let's start by recognizing the Occupy Archive as a starting point for the process of investigation. Let's identify it first and foremost as place and instrument of knowledge production rather than information retrieval, and as a site that is embedded within specific institutional (government) bureaucracies and socio-political infrastructures, practices of resistance, and historical narratives.

This book is also the product of a network of different relationships. My main adviser throughout the research phase was Amy Roberts. Roberts is a New York-based activist-archivist who co-founded the Occupy Wall Street Archives Working Group with Jeremy Bold, who was employed at the Elmer Holmes Bobst Library at New York University.[13] Roberts has also been the collection's long-term custodian. She and I have very different relationships with the Occupy Archive. The collection was, for me, a starting point, and the nearly three-year process of negotiation that was required to gain access to the Tamiment Library collections gave me some insight into and experience of the challenges and complexities surrounding the affiliation of Occupy with a formal institution. My research process was characterized by delay after delay, such that this book (which had initially been designed as the first publication within *The Disobedient Museum* trilogy) came to be known as 'The Impossible Project'. During the course of the research I was periodically granted access to a series of related materials, including a different archive of internal documents and correspondences between Archives Working Group members. The email trails and other forms of communication in the separate collections demonstrate the life cycle of the Archives Working Group and its fraught interactions with the General Assembly, and I realized that the 'impossible project' was a term that aptly described their experience, particularly given that the collection did not end up being fully acquired by Tamiment Library until 2018.

I was not alone in equating the archives project with impossibility.[14] In response to the question, 'What did you think were the biggest challenges and limitations faced by the Archives Working Group in realizing its mission?' one member replied: 'Challenging traditional practices of constructing history by documenting an ongoing event in the present. It was a seemingly impossible task, but resonant with the visionary nature of OWS in trying to imagine a world that was impossible' (see Roberts n.d.h: 17). This response was reiterated by others as a key feature of the movement, and came to have a central place in the philosophy adopted by the group: 'I don't fault the Working Group for thinking big and dreaming big. I think it was part and parcel of being part of any kind of movement', said another member: 'You wouldn't start a movement if you didn't think that moving mountains was possible. You don't think small, people' (see Roberts n.d.h: 22).

For Roberts, the collection is both a means and an end point; an assemblage that embodies the actions and interactions that led to its creation. Her role as co-creator of the Archives Working Group means her view about where this book should start emphasizes the process that encapsulated the aspirations and actions of the Archives group, rather than with the collection it produced. Toward late September 2011, in the early days of the Occupy encampment, Roberts wrote in her working notebook that the story should start like this:

> Go and document history as it happens. In the Archives working group we're also archiving ourselves as participants. No such thing as objective or unbiased archiving. Our archive project reflects challenges of this movement and this society.
>
> (Roberts n.d.f)

While Roberts' and my engagement with the Occupy Wall Street movement and the events represented in the archive have different start and end points, this book reflects our shared understanding of the subject status – and indeed, subjectivity – of the collection.

Roberts' statement summarizes the key elements, challenges, and significance of the collection for her as a producer working within and across various communities of practice. Her statement has, through the course of the research, come to have a central role in my analysis of contemporary activist archiving and the interaction between museums and collecting institutions and social reform movements. For both of us the collection is less important as a cohort of physical items that exist as the material residue of the Occupy Wall Street movement than it is evidence of a process of meaning-making. We both identify as critical to the collection's value the fact that it has existed itself as a site of resistance that exemplifies many of the fundamental challenges and limitations – as well as opportunities – that existed at the heart of the Occupy Wall Street movement and that are also, incidentally, increasingly valued by proponents of activist collecting, archiving, and scholarship.

Parameters of study

Contemporary cause-based collecting and analysis (both of *and through* contemporary cause-based collections) and the socio-political relevance of these activities are central to this book. In it, I explore a series of collections, the majority of which are now held at the Tamiment Library and Robert F. Wagner Labor Archives at New York University. I argue that the collection cannot be analyzed in isolation from the contexts and period in which it was developed. This approach to collections analysis requires identifying the utility of the archive as a resource as well as engaging with and understanding how it functions as an agentic subject that was developed out of the intention to influence the public sphere. I also recognize the significance of input from the Occupy Wall Street Archives Working Group, particularly the work undertaken by the participants most directly involved in the production of the collection.

The study begins chronologically, by recognizing the Zuccotti Park occupation as a site and event (from September 17, 2011), which led to the establishment of the Archives Working Group at Liberty Plaza 'about a week after the occupation began' on September 24 (Roberts n.d.c; Evans, Perricci, and Roberts 2014).[15] The second phase focuses on the transformation of the organizational structures of the Occupy movement as it developed following the police raids throughout the winter of 2011 and 2012, during which meetings were held at the atrium at 60 Wall Street.[16] The third phase extends from the second through to mid-2017, and covers the process by which the collection was finally accessioned by the Tamiment Library and Robert F. Wagner Labor Archives at New York University.

My approach to analyzing the collection created by the Occupy Wall Street Archives Working Group was to start with a preliminary survey of representative collections of Occupy Wall Street materials. I restricted my attention to the occupation of Zuccotti Park from September 11 to November 15. It was not my aim to develop a comprehensive audit of Occupy materials,[17] and I applied a narrow lens to focus on the Tamiment collection at the expense of other surveyed collections. I excluded a number of collections from the study, including the small, bespoke collection held at the Museum of the City of New York. Developed as the result of a call for material donations that the museum extended to all New Yorkers rather than occupiers specifically, this collection was made to fill several deficiencies existing in the museum's late twentieth-century social movement collections (Chapin 2017). Created in line with the museum's mission to preserve and present the history of New York City and its people (Ott 2016),[18] it was created after the Zuccotti Park occupation had been dispersed. The museum's strategic reason for developing the small collection is evident in the mode of acquisition as well as the small number of items that were acquired. The materials are currently held within the museum's education collection and it presents a social justice story that links to other themes including feminism and women's reproductive rights. It did not require donors to have had any affiliation with the movement (although all items selected were 'pro' Occupy) and does not reflect an interest in self-representation.

The Museum of the City of New York collection is further distinguished from that at Tamiment Library by being starkly, almost forensically clean and orderly, both in its cataloguing and its physicality. Much more 'readable' (open to comprehension) than those at Tamiment Library, it produces a narrative that provides a coherent picture of an episode in the history of the city, rather than the urgent experience that is evoked by the uniformly dirty, crumpled and water-damaged records at Tamiment. I also excluded an equally modest collection held at the Smithsonian Institution, which was made by a long-time curator at the National Museum of American History's Division of Political History, Barbara Clark (2016).[19] Reports of 'helicopter collecting', whereby a representative from an institution descends, obtains materials, and returns to their establishment, exist about the attendance of Smithsonian curators at Occupy Wall Street, who reportedly collected a small number of items that were felt to have the potential for gaining national significance in the long term.[20]

The collections now held at Tamiment Library are referred to collectively throughout this book as the 'Occupy Archive'. They are examples of self-representation and activist archiving.[21] They demonstrate a different development approach than those employed by the Museum of the City of New York and the Smithsonian Institution's collections, which I use a thematic label to refer to, following Bold (2012a), as the 'OWS archives'. The participant-driven approach to collection development embodied by the Occupy Archive has greater affinities with a third collection, which I survey only briefly. Located in Brooklyn, Interference Archive provides a community-focused form of activist archiving.[22] Despite growing out of the Occuprint Group associated with Occupy Wall Street in 2011 and having close ties to the Archives Working Group and the Library Working Group, it privileges a general narrative interpretation of social justice over the specificities of the experience of Occupy Wall Street participants. One working group member describes differences in the ways that the Archives Working Group and other established institutions approached the process of archiving Occupy Wall Street:

> With the exception of Tamiment archives, archival repositories stepped in briefly to collect items of interest. [In contrast] the working group worked as embedded archivists, witnessing important events, recording the perspective of participants, creating and collecting documents that would otherwise have been missed by the outside repositories. It also attempted to coordinate the efforts of individual archivists through consensus processes that were applied by other OWS working groups.
> (See Roberts n.d.h: 11)

In emphasizing the curatorial role of bearing witness, this statement differentiates the collecting framework employed by the Archives Working Group from the approach employed by other institutions acquiring materials from the event.

In addition, rather than having a singular focus – to represent, for example, the movement's interaction with or significance for the city (as per the Museum of the City of New York), nation (as per the Smithsonian Institution), or social justice theme (as per the Interference Archive) – the remit of the Archives Working Group was open and inclusive.[23] Working group members did not determine value according to monetary worth or even temporal longevity; a point which was fiercely debated within the group.[24] Neither did they employ the parameters for collecting which are normally included in institutional collecting policies. They did undertake to include 'documents about the decision making processes of Occupy Wall Street, of the General Assembly, Coordinators, Think Tank, and Occupiers' meetings, as well as the records of the other subgroups'. Their mission statement explains the aim to 'guarantee that OWS remain a transparent movement'. A central focus was on presenting and reflecting on the role the collection could play in ensuring 'the accountability of OWS by documenting our ideas, ideals, strategies, structure, tactics, politics, and culture of OWS and the ways it has helped reshape the political discourse in New York, the nation, and the world' (Roberts 2011a).

About this book

The collection at the heart of this book has two formal typological components, which are categorized materially by Tamiment Library. The first part of the collection is made up of object-based materials that were typically produced to represent the claims of the Occupy Wall Street movement (primarily picket signs, buttons, banners, and other disposable items used in protests and rallies). The second part is constituted by documentary (primarily paper-based) elements that reflect the organizational and communication processes occurring internally within the Occupy Archives Working Group (diaries, memos, meeting minutes, and the like, which recorded the formation of the movement's organizational structures). This formal categorization has been echoed in the overarching structure of this book. The first half focuses on the object-based collections, which are framed in relation to an exercise asking what the objects tell us about the Occupy Wall Street movement. What account of Occupy is narrated by this collection of attention-grabbing materials? The second part of the book investigates the documentary materials, which are framed in relation to the question of what participants thought and how they tried to influence the actions and internal politics of the prefigurative political movement they participated in.

My key observations come together by arguing that the collections at the heart of the book (both object- and text-based) are an autoethnographic record that was produced collectively by members of the Archives Working Group. The approach taken by working group members to contemporary cause-based collecting was autoethnographic (Maréchal 2010; Adams, Holman Jones, and Ellis 2015: 2; Ellis, Adams, and Bochner 2010) and political in that it rejected the objective distance associated with traditional forms of ethnography (by and about 'others'). Their approach aimed to wrest control from institutions including established museums, archives, and libraries that have often historically functioned as repositories for ethnographic principles and narratives (Chang 2008).

Beyond the immediate parameters and contents of the collections, the book is informed by and seeks to continue *The Disobedient Museum* trilogy's interest in engaging with, articulating, and modeling methodological approaches to examine the strengths and limitations of disciplinary and interdisciplinary practices for writing resistance. It extends the discussion of activist writing represented in *The Disobedient Museum*, which advocates for writing that acts itself as a political statement in addition to offering a process for the examination of such (Message 2018a: 2). It also presents a current-day bookend for my previous investigations into historical examples of contemporary cause-based collecting from the perspective of institutionally based curators (Message 2014; Message 2018b).[25] Finally, it offers an account of my and Roberts' roles in undertaking an exchange between a researcher and activist archivist, which might be considered as constituting a further phase in the collection's formation and, or transformation of meaning. The book seeks to conduct a material analysis that occurs 'from the inside out *and* the outside in: a partnership, respectively and ideally, of archivists and historians, for they both have much to teach each other' (Cook 2011: 623). It recognizes the argument that was made by another member of the working group during an interview conducted by Roberts:

> While historical accounts (books) and theory (books) play an important role in shaping the experience of a social movement (and those active in the movement) most activists play a larger role in constructing (often accidentally) the material that will one day wind up in the archive as opposed to actually using the archives. Nevertheless the archives become important repositories for the long-term memory of the movement as they provide the source material for new histories to be constructed off of the old movements. Or to sum up, memory is extremely important and archives may convey this memory, but for most activists 'archives' appears at a sort of academic distance from the reality of their day-to-day activism. Granted all of this is different when talking specifically to activist/radical archives where the very act of archiving may be a manifestation of the social movement.
>
> (See Roberts n.d.h: 11)

In the final instance, this book has two goals. The first is to make a contribution to the body of knowledge, including the historical and contemporary discourses and future practices of activism (social movement studies). The second is to enhance understandings about activist collecting and archiving for the benefit of archive and museum studies and related fields, and to model ways that scholars from these fields might *write activism*.

Chapter outline

Working within this overarching content-directed structure and theoretical context, the book's central investigation is framed around the guiding questions of when, where, who, what, how, and why that guided the Archives Working Group's approach to building, reflecting on, and advocating for its collection (Roberts n.d.d).[26] Extending from this introduction's preliminary account of the when, where, and who relevant for this study, Chapter 1, 'Activist collecting: Writing movement lives through things', starts by describing what I mean by the Occupy Archive in relation to other collections and archives. It provides a brief overview of parallel archives constituted by cognate activist collection activities and explores the intentions of the Archives Working Group in developing their collection. Its central argument is that the material residue of social reform movements provides a unique and understudied form of narrative representation.[27] Focused on an exploration of the collections development work and the autoethnographic processes undertaken by the working group, it describes the parameters for the collections analysis at the heart of this book.

Chapter 2, 'Object lessons: Occupy Wall Street. Bring tent', focuses on how the collection described in Chapter 1 represents the Occupy Wall Street movement. It models a process of collection analysis that focuses on the object histories that emerge from a specific subsection of the Occupy Archive. The collection of placards and signs used in protests and marches throughout Occupy Wall Street were identified for this exercise because I wanted to target materials that lend themselves easily to narrative interpretation. The descriptive and interpretive approach also aims to clearly represent the links between material culture produced by participants and the broader field of political action and information within which the materials were produced.

Chapter 3, 'Organizing action: Archiving Occupy', examines why the Archives Working Group was committed to creating a material record of the movement from 'the inside'. It examines the role archives played in the context of creating historical narratives for, of, and about the nascent Occupy Wall Street movement and the organizational forms the movement sought to establish. It also assesses the internal politics represented by the collection, investigating how it reflects the misunderstandings and conflict between the Archives Working Group and the Occupy Wall Street New York City General Assembly.[28] This chapter's evaluation broadens the focus from key collections at Tamiment Library to include observation of a non-object-based digital archive of personal communications that may more easily be understood as 'subjective'. The analysis undertaken in this chapter leads to observations about the lack of value attributed to culture in the context of social movement politics generally. It explores the role of internal activism as a way of advocating the benefits of activist archiving to the broader Occupy Wall Street movement. The book's short conclusion gives an overview of the contribution that the Occupy Archive has made to understandings about activism and archiving respectively. It also provides a brief summation of the role that this book has played in the broader context of *The Disobedient Museum* trilogy.

Conclusion: The 99% occupy the archive

The material records and physicality of individual items within the Occupy Archive are of key importance to this book, and I am not suggesting that the collection's subjectivity (object status) can or should be distanced from the function of the archive as a source of evidence. The working notebook cited earlier (which is also the source for this introduction's title) is one of a series of such journals included in the collections and written by Roberts, a prolific note-taker. It is just one of the hundreds of first-person accounts and appeals represented in accounts, letters, manifestos, postage delivery labels, Christmas cards, food package notes, etc. that the Occupy Archive includes to represent the 99%. While the lack of organization of the collections (roughly chronological, with estimated dates indicated by handwritten sticky notes) would make its semiotics challenging if not impenetrable without some knowledge of and reference to an external context, the notebooks provide a narrative spine for the collection as well as a means for understanding the processes of archiving the Occupy movement.

It would be incorrect to designate the notebooks as a series. Rather, the collection includes a number of books and writing pads of different types, sizes, and page numbers, such as personal diaries, calendars, tiny flip-back Spirax pads, and address books, which have been grabbed and repurposed. These 'notebooks' (also too coherent a descriptor) are covered in dark, firmly pressed handwriting that responds to and records events and meeting minutes, as well as the plans and frustrations of the Archives Working Group. At times, the pen – or sometimes a faint blunt pencil – has been used so firmly that it has torn holes through the paper. The books do not have designated start and end dates, and it is possible that notes were being written across more than one 'volume' consecutively. It is possible to work out their dates by cross-referencing against other materials. The physicality of the notebooks and other items exist as both an evidence source of information and as an experience critical for any attempt to engage meaningfully with the Occupy Archive as a form of direct action and a documentary record of events.

Notes

1 Roberts (n.d.f).
2 Occupy Wall Street (OWS) was a leaderless left-wing protest movement that began in New York's financial district on September 17, 2011. Its most defining characteristics were a decentralized organizational model and a commitment to participatory, consensus-based decision-making. Its methods included physical occupations, civil disobedience, picketing, demonstrations, and internet activism. The movement refused to be pinned down to any single cause or goal, but the range of issues it represented rallied against the social and economic

inequality caused by political corruption and corporate influence over government. The Occupy movement quickly mushroomed throughout the US and globally, and when protesters were forced out of Zuccotti Park on November 15, 2011, they turned their focus to occupying banks, corporate headquarters, board meetings, foreclosed homes, and college and university campuses.

3 Message field notes, July 4, 2018.

4 A press release issued by the Smithsonian Institution's National Museum of American History on January 23, 2017, articulated the museum's rationale for collecting material to document a range of events and political persuasions, including Trump's presidential inauguration, the 2017 Women's March on Washington, and other protest actions. It said these events are:

> part of the Museum's long tradition of documenting how Americans participate in the political process and how citizens exercise their first amendment rights of assembly and free speech. The Museum collects from contemporary events because many of these materials are ephemeral and if not collected immediately are lost to the historical record.
>
> (Smithsonian National Museum of American History 2017)

5 The history of contemporary cause-based collecting includes actions by institutions acquiring materials from political campaigns, elections, and other processes. It also covers the emergence of crisis-based collecting from natural disasters and man-made catastrophes such as 9/11 (Message 2014; Message 2018a; Gardner 2015; Gardner 2016).

6 Message field notes, July 4, 2018.

7 According to Stoler, anthropologists:

> engaged in post-colonial studies are increasingly adopting an historical perspective and using archives. Yet their archival activity tends to remain more an extractive than an ethnographic one. Documents are thus still invoked piecemeal to confirm the colonial invention of certain practices or to underscore cultural claims, silent. Yet such mining of the content of government commissions, reports, and other archival sources rarely pays attention to their peculiar placement and form. Scholars need to move from archive-as-source to archive-as-subject.
>
> (Stoler 2002: 87)

8 This model continues to exist as fundamentally useful, see Appadurai and Breckenridge (1992); also discussed in Message (2018a: 48).

9 An indication of the role that inclusion had in the working group is provided by one working group member's response to the question 'What role do you think archives and memory can have in social movements?' She said:

> I think it's really easy when involved in any movement to gloss over the important histories of those movements and what I think of is feminism, and just see this master narrative and not think about all the ruptures and the points where there were differing opinions. ... and I like differing movements within a broader umbrella movement and I think that it is really important for something like Occupy to remember that it's not just this single unified thing

and it's so easy to look at history that way that's what archives do; it's like the physical evidence of these counter-narratives.

(See Roberts n.d.h: 17)

10   104 NYCGA (New York City General Assembly)-affiliated working groups are listed at www.nycga.net/documents/GROUP DOCUMENTS (last accessed August 10, 2016, link no longer live). Some of these included: Town Planning, Art and Culture, Legal, Sanitation, Medical, Outreach, Comfort, Kitchen, Treasury, Media, Direct Action, Jail Support, Tech Ops, and Facilitation. A directory of Occupy sites was also previously available at http://www.directory.occupy.net.

11   Talking about what he called 'the situation' of the Occupy experience, one working group member explained:

> One of the problems, was that like, I frequently personally ran into my fellow activists and like, we don't live in the world that our prefigurative utopian friends dreamed up and we can have this "Beautiful Open access Archival Space where we can just put all of this and it will be wonderful!" And you kind of have to think about the real situation. ... But especially from an archival perspective, you've got to make realistic decisions based on what you have. And based on the situation. ... I mean, this is an imperfect situation and you were making an imperfect decision, and guess what, that's called archiving.
>
> (See Roberts n.d.h: 15)

12   The internal working documents and notes in the Occupy Archive reflect a view that the movement was grappling with how a new form of horizontal 'order' might be applied: 'You can organize things horizontally and still have things organized', said one member (see Roberts n.d.h: 28).

13   Written on the inside cover of one notebook is the following 'Bio: Amy Roberts is a graduate student; studying archives and library science at Queens College ... and started the Occupy Wall Street Archives working group interested in documenting the movement as it takes place and as participants' (Roberts n.d.f).

14   Reference to the impossibility of the archiving project is also a recurring feature of communications by members of the Archives Working Group. For example, in a call for participants to attend a public forum on February 5, 2011, on the topic of 'What should an archive of Occupy Wall Street look like?' the text says: 'on its surface, it appears to be an impossible task: to document the activities of a major social movement as it is happening' (Ng 2012a). Several members of the working group also use the term in separate interviews with Roberts (see Roberts n.d.h: 20; Roberts n.d.d). In addition, 'impossible' was also used as an adjective by activists to describe the broader Occupy movement. Notably David Graeber called consensus-based decision-making a process of 'enacting the impossible' that would, nonetheless, be achievable within the movement (Graeber 2011: n.p.; Mitchell 2012: 14).

15   There are different opinions about the commencement of, and precedents for Occupy Wall Street and its attention to public relations communication approaches. Mitchell argues, for example, that

> at the level of the imaginary, which is to say the level of media spectacle and widely shared images of reality, the revolution of our moment did not

begin on September 17 with the Adbusters call to Occupy Wall Street. It had already begun in the United States with the iconography of the Tea Party, and the effort to stage a populist and nationalist revival around images of the original American Revolution.

(Mitchell 2013b: 98)

My account of Occupy is contextualized and bookended by my earlier analysis of a Tea Party rally and iconography relative to the interests of this book series (Message 2018a).

16 60 Wall Street is the national headquarters for Deutsche Bank in the US and also holds a subway station. Its atrium, which a journalist called 'The Real Headquarters of OWS' (Gimein 2011), is, like Zuccotti Park, a privately owned public space (or 'POPS'), which means it has been zoned as an amenity provided and maintained by a private owner or developer for public use. POPS can be external or internal spaces, plazas, arcades, or even residential lobbies. For an overview, history, and standards in New York City see https://www1.nyc.gov/site/planning/plans/pops/pops.page.

17 Other collections that would be valuable for further investigation include the Roy Rosenzweig Center for History and New Media at George Mason University, although the *Economist* (A. T. 2011) reported that they were mostly interested in digital materials, as was the Internet Archive (available at https://archive.org/details/occupywallstreet). I have also wondered what might remain of the NY Police Department holdings and whether anything has been transferred to the Police Museum or archives. Digital archives and materials are discussed further in Evans, Perricci, and Roberts (2014).

18 Even at the time at which the Occupy materials were acquired, there was no formal collection policy regarding cause-based materials. Interim collecting guidelines had been approved by the institution's Collections Committee, meaning that while staff could not actively seek materials to add to the collection, they were able to consider materials offered by individuals on a case-by-case basis (Chapin 2017; also see the museum's mission statement at https://www.mcny.org).

19 Mystery existed around the collecting activities and possible (unlikely) 'alleged collaboration with Smithsonian' and someone–called Tommy Knox (or sometimes, 'Tommy Fox'). His presence at Liberty Plaza was noted in minutes from a meeting of the Archives Working Group (Roberts n.d.g), and reported by journalist, Michelle Dean (2001), who says he was referred to as 'The Rogue Archivist'. Collecting for the Smithsonian was small scale and informal but undertaken with institutional support. It was guided by the aim to find representative items that would complement the museum's existing collection of protest materials and stand the test of time in terms of conservation and clarity (Clark 2016).

20 Valeska M. Hilbig, Deputy Director of Public Affairs at the Smithsonian, was reported as referring

to a museum statement that puts the initiative in the context of similar recent efforts. 'The protests are still ongoing, and things are still unfolding,' Ms. Hilbig told the *Washington Times*. 'Historians like to take the long view and see how things play out. They wouldn't feel comfortable to discuss it until they have had a chance to get the historic perspective'.

(Flamini 2011)

21 Donated by Amy Roberts of the Occupy Wall Street Archives Working Group, in 2013 and 2017. Additional materials associated with the collection were found in the repository in April 2014. In August 2017, 17 items were prepared to be moved to offsite art storage. In September 2017, the ephemera, letters of support, diary, organizational documents, periodicals, and some posters were housed in archival folders and boxes. Materials were kept in the broad categories in which they were arranged when received from the donor. The placards, signs, drums, and textiles were not processed at that time. In January 2018, additional ephemera, letters of support, diaries, organizational documents, periodicals, and posters were added to the collection. Information about this collection is available at http://dlib.nyu.edu/findingaids/html/tamwag/tam_630/tam_630.html.

22 Materials donated from the Archives Working Group to Interference Archive in Brooklyn include ephemera, posters (some made by Occuprint member Josh Macphee, who co-founded Interference Archive with Dara Greenwald, Molly Fair, and Kevin Caplicki) and publications, as well as the Born Digital Collection from the Archives Working Group. The Interference Archive mission statement says:

> We use this cultural ephemera to animate histories of people mobilizing for social transformation. We consider the use of our collection to be a way of preserving and honoring histories and material culture that is often marginalized in mainstream institutions.
>
> (Available at http://interferencearchive.org/our-mission/)

23 The Archives Working Group was organized like most other working groups in the Occupy movement, with open membership and consensus-based decision-making processes. Attendance at the meetings and participation in their decision-making processes was available to all. As well as holding regular meetings, they encouraged wide participation in their decision-making processes by holding public forums at which attendees debated how archives should be managed and where they should be stored ('OWS Archives Budget Proposal' 2012; Ng 2012a; Ng 2012b).

24 'If we had more time and resources, we would have tried to determine which objects have intrinsic value and which don't' (Evans, Perricci, and Roberts 2014).

25 I have not included lengthy discussion about the differences in categories, definitions and practices between archives and museums, preferring to instead focus on the actions undertaken. For a survey of definitional approaches see Dudley (2012). See Message (2018a) for explanation about the expansive approach to defining 'museum' that I have employed in this book. For an argument on the 'obvious, and instructive' parallels between museums and archives, see Schwartz and Cook (2002: 8). Where possible, I follow the nomenclature of the working group, and use the terms 'collections' and 'archives' interchangeably to describe material assemblages.

26 This approach also acknowledges the first-hand contribution of the chapter written by working group members, Evans, Perricci, and Roberts (2014), which is structured as a response to queries including 'Why Archive? And Other Important Questions Asked by Occupiers'.

27 I take my understanding of narrative from Peter Goldie, who says:

> A narrative is a representation of events that is shaped, organized, and coloured, presenting those events and the people involved in them from a certain perspective or perspectives and, thereby, giving narrative structure – coherence, meaningfulness, and evaluative and emotional import – to what is narrated.
>
> (Goldie 2012: 8)

The relevance of this definition for object-based stories has also been discussed in Brown *et al.* (2015: 20–21).

28 One indication of these issues, which are analyzed in Chapter 3, are suggested in Roberts' statement that 'Organizational problems are political problems' (Roberts n.d.c).

1 Activist collecting

Writing movement lives through things

When I talk about 'a collection' in this book, I am primarily referring to the official 'Occupy Archive' at Tamiment Library/Robert F. Wagner Labor Archives (Tamiment Library and Robert F. Wagner Labor Archive 2018). For the pragmatic reason that it has distinct parameters that facilitate the making of observations, my efforts at collections analysis are restricted to that physical assemblage unless otherwise stated. At times I do extend my analysis to include a number of collateral or comparative collections that are conceptually cognate or related to my principal case study, but not held by Tamiment Library. These collections are collectively referred to as the 'OWS archives'. My approach recognizes Bold's argument that 'it is incorrect to refer to this collection [at Tamiment] as "the" OWS Archives collection, especially as respects the fact that many collections of OWS materials exist' (Bold 2012a).[1] Debates about whether the Tamiment collection does or does not constitute the sole or singular Occupy Wall Street Archives highlights internal debates within the Archives Working Group about ownership of the materials.[2] These debates also reflect contention over the fact that although this collection was created by the Occupy Wall Street Archives Working Group, it is now located externally, even if partially, at Tamiment Library.[3] In the final instance, I distinguish the Tamiment collection (the Occupy Archive) from the wider cohort of Occupy collections (the OWS archives) throughout the book, but present the Tamiment collection as offering a representative physical assemblage of Occupy materials such that this distinction is more semantic than particularly significant.

My interest in researching the collection is guided by the aim to describe how the processes and actions of the Occupy Wall Street Archives Working Group – as embodied in the collections they created – contributed to the movement as a whole. Much of the material culture 'repatriated' from Liberty Plaza is now held within collections at Tamiment Library, described by the institution's finding aid in the following way:

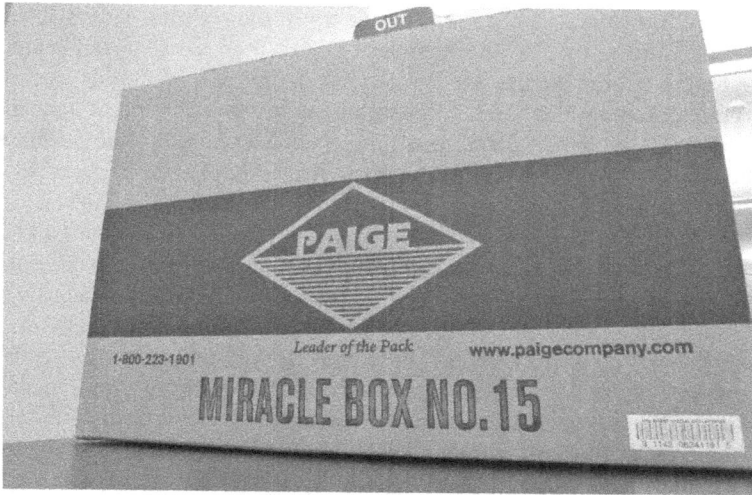

Figure 1.1 Archive box, Occupy Wall Street Archives Working Group Records, TAM 630, Tamiment Library/Robert F. Wagner Labor Archives, New York University.

Photograph by Kylie Message.

The Occupy Wall Street Archives Working Group Records document protests by the Occupy movement between 2011 and 2013, and the work of the Archives Working Group (AWG) to collect materials from these protests. The bulk of the collection documents the first Occupy Wall Street (OWS) protest in the fall of 2011 in Zuccotti Park in Manhattan, New York. Materials include placards, signs, fliers, artwork, clippings from print and online news sources, letters of support, diaries, periodicals, pamphlets, music, born-digital photographs, material from the Occupy Wall Street Library, stickers, buttons, textiles with protest slogans, notebooks, correspondence, organizational documents, and the movement's newsletter, *The Occupied Wall Street Journal*. The ephemera, clippings, pamphlets, and periodicals document Occupy, climate change, and racial justice protests in New York, Massachusetts, and Pennsylvania. The placards and signs were created by members of the OWS movement in Zuccotti Park in 2011 and document the main issues of the movement, in particular income inequality, wealth distribution, and the influence of corporations on the government. The ephemera includes buttons, fliers, and posters. Artwork includes large and small scale pieces, including two one dollar bills with protest slogans stamped on them, casino chips with protest slogans, and posters. The letters of support are letters from friends and family of the members of OWS in Lower Manhattan, supporters from across the country, and one seventh grade social studies class in New Jersey. Some of the letters contained financial donations, food, gift cards, and other items supporters thought may be of use to the members of the movement. The diaries contain personal entries and meeting notes created by unidentified members of the Occupy movement. The notebooks were found in Zuccotti Park after a raid on the protesters by the New York Police Department in November 2011 and collected by members of the Archives Working Group. The organizational documents include draft vision statements, a "Declaration of the Occupation of New York City", meeting agenda and notes, and notes taken by Amy Roberts at working group meetings. The working groups documented in this collection include the Archives Working Group and the Music Working Group, with some unspecified working groups. The born-digital photographs depict protesters and police officers, the signs provide information for members of the protest, and the music is a CD with the song "People's Park". Material documenting the AWG includes mission statements, draft budget proposals, meeting agenda, minutes, and notes. The bulk of the AWG records consist of notes taken by Roberts at AWG meetings, with other material consisting of budget proposals presented to the OWS General Assembly and notes on collecting oral histories and archives best practices.

(Tamiment Library and Robert F. Wagner
Labor Archive 2018)

Members of the Archives Working Group used the materiality of the collection to 'increase our visibility to others in this movement' (Roberts n.d.c). The group's aim was to improve the movement's support of their work. As with all presentations to the General Assembly, their opportunities for attention were brief and needed to be translated across a large and diverse crowd using the hand gesture communication techniques employed by Occupy (Hand gesture palm card descriptors 2011; also Hudgins 2011a). This support and the subsequent approvals it engendered was not a 'nice to have' optional feature of Occupy. It was a necessity. Without the full backing required for consensus, their proposals for funding for storage and preservation for the materials were rejected. In one public forum that sought to increase understanding about how material items embodied the fundamental ideological premise of Occupy, Roberts' incorporated props into her presentation:

Here's an item! Look at what this sign is made out of. It's a reclaimed orange police net.

(Roberts n.d.k)

Resist, reclaim, recreate [is] what occupy means. Reclaim ideas, space, definitions and meaning. What an orange police net signifies is not entrapment. A lot of these signs were made from this orange net. This sign says 'Screw you to the police.'

(Roberts n.d.k)

The orange net became a central signifier for the Archives Working Group.[4] In re-using it for attention, the group came to identify its potential value in connecting their commitment to the cause with that of other working groups. It is a recurring emblem in many speeches, including at a 'Public Forum on the OWS Archives' held February 5 that asked 'What should an archive of Occupy Wall Street look like?' (Ng 2012a). It was also used at an OWS Archives Share Day, on March 31, 2012 (Ng 2012b). Roberts opened the discussion at this event by saying

I'd like to draw people's attention to this orange net that says Info and Media on it. People from OWS will remember these signs were all over the park to show where Kitchen, Medical, Arts & Culture, Media, Sanitation were in the park. This is an incredibly unique arti-fact for many reasons. This material that the signs were made out of came from the orange police nets that the police use during mass arrests.

(Roberts n.d.c)

The Archives Working Group articulated a clear belief in the activist role of archiving and of the contribution that the collection would make to the movement. They aimed to assert self-determination and control over the material products and memory of the movement, and to assert author-ship over the way in which the movement was included in an historical context (Roberts n.d.g).[5] The key purpose of the Archives Working Group was to:

- Go document history as it happens.
- W/the archive working group we're also archiving ourselves as participants.
- no such thing as objective or unbiased archiving.
- Our archive project reflects the challenges of this mvmt [move-ment] and this society. (Roberts n.d.f)

Working group members did not attempt to be neutral observers, and had to balance their documentation and collection activities with the daily operations, actions, and training sessions of Occupy.[6] As such, they explained their aim as being twofold: creating a collection and organizing politically (Roberts n.d.g). The intersection of the two informed their actions as explained by one set of notes that considers how to simultaneously contribute to the movement and collect various items including, in one instance, the painted umbrellas used as props in one direct action: 'Should we try to go inside and risk arrest?' ... 'better to stay outside and do outreach? Is it a better use of resources? Do speak-outs' (Roberts n.d.g, *emphasis in original*).

Central to the task of collections analysis presented throughout this book is the understanding that, like the act of creating an activist archive, the act of analyzing one is not unbiased. A 'subjective' approach to collections analysis seeks to makes explicit the human relationships embedded within the materials, as well as those generated subsequently by, as well as those missing from, the collection.[7] It draws from Star's (1999: 379) work on systems, which informs an understanding of archives as being more than a sum of their parts, with the potential to play critical roles in the shape and experience of other adjacent knowledge systems they interact with, inform, and are influenced by. Work by Star and others referenced here (Stoler 2002) acknowledge a theoretical genealogy that includes Foucault and Derrida, amongst others, who have argued that archives are 'neither passive or value free but rather serve as active sites where social power is negotiated, controlled and confirmed' (Schwartz and Cook 2002: 1). For example, identification of the interaction – and subjectivity that can guide interactions – between content, collection, and context is also fundamental for any attempt to pursue Stoler's (2010) project of engaging with archives as primary subjects rather than as secondary contexts.

This chapter starts by explaining 'what' the collection at the heart of this study is. From here I offer an overview of the historical context for activist collecting before moving on to examine some of the motivations and methodologies employed by working group members in regard to the development of the collection. The final section considers the subjective nature of collecting, and some of the first-person stories that contributed to and are represented within the Occupy Archive. I conclude by making some comments about the contribution that material and archival case studies can offer to political discourse and the field of social movement studies.

Contemporary cause-based collecting

In an interview with Roberts (as interviewer) in 2013, one working group member said that in his view – as a member of Occupy who was also a professional archivist – the intentions and collections of the Archives Working Group were 'precedent-setting'. He recognized the contribution that the collection makes to the profession of archiving and to the related field of historical knowledge. He also made a critical association between what the Archives Working Group sought to do and other historical examples of cause-based collecting:

> And I will say this about the collection, to give you and the rest of the folks in the working group and in the movement credit. The collection exists because of what you guys did. And that accomplishment should not be underestimated. The fact that there is an OWS collection that was collected and gathered by and within the movement, I think it's precedent setting. Again I leave that up to you and your research to look at other social and grassroots movements to say who else has done something like this in a contemporary fashion. 'You know there's 40 years since that March on Washington and I wonder what's in my old shoe box, maybe I should give it to them.' You know, that and the fact that I don't know what the linear cubic footage is but it's not small. It's not a box. It's not two boxes. There is weight and substance to it for future historians to use and for a good purpose. But I think, from what I've seen of it, I think you accomplished the mission statement – to self-document, absolutely.
>
> (See Roberts n.d.h: 24)[8]

Contemporary cause-based collections can be defined as groups of materials acquired from social movements, usually in collaboration with participants, or through a process of self-documentation by members of the movement. In *Museums and Social Activism* (2014), I investigated the occurrence of contemporary cause-based collecting at the National Museum of American History from the mid- to late 1960s, arguing that the activities of Smithsonian Institution curators Keith Melder and Edie Mayo were precedent setting in their interest in representing key social movements (including the 1963 March on Washington for Jobs and Freedom mentioned by interviewee above; also see Message 2014: 24). While collecting from social reform movements has become an almost ubiquitous requirement for museums, archives, and other collecting repositories today, there remains a difference between the ways they typically go about this task and how movements are represented in self-collected, if not independent, archives.

The practices and protocols pioneered by Melder and Mayo remained firmly aligned with an institutional perspective,[9] yet they were also committed to the practice of curatorial activism that was sometimes at odds with the agenda or procedures of the museum in which they were employed. They both made significant contributions to the discourse around contemporary collecting that is also evident in the work of the Occupy Wall Street Archives Working Group, many of whom were professional or student archivists. However, despite sharing comparable motivations and aims, archival activism appears to have developed alongside rather than in alliance with museological collecting practices. This means that the previous statement about the working group being precedent setting is accurate, but that it is also useful to examine some of the similarities that exist with previous curatorial attempts at collecting social reform movements, if for no other reason than they can provide further insight into and a chronology for the difficulties that established institutions can face with collecting this material. After all, these reasons were an important part of why the Archives Working Group sought to protect the movement's own versions, voices, authority, and independence over that of a host institution.

The legacy of cause-based collecting to which Melder, Mayo, and others contributed further indicates the impossibility of separating the personal from the political in the Occupy Archive, and the interpersonal from the institutional in the context of activist collecting more generally. This is as evident in the approach to collecting taken by the Archives Working Group as it was by Mayo over 40 years earlier, when she said:

> Because I find the most effective contact to be a personal one, I have begun attending a rally or protest, or participating in the activity. If you are fortunate enough to establish rapport with someone in the group, zero in on the items you want. ... If you are working on a specific exhibit for which objects are needed, offer your contact the prospect of imminent display of his material. It is often hazardous to collect at such demonstrations, but from such collecting forays have come our most valuable 'movement' materials – hats, posters and organizational materials from Resurrection City; posters, literature and banners from anti-Vietnam war demonstrations, American Indian Movement demands and literature from the occupation of the Bureau of Indian Affairs; and impeachment materials.
>
> (Mayo quoted in Message 2014: 81)

The main distinction, of course, is that Mayo remained self-identified as a representative of her institution whereas the Occupy Archive represented the movement as insiders. Mayo's role as a curator at a national museum was to collect materials that were meaningful to a national imaginary, rather than those depicting state, regional, or cause-based issues. Although Mayo advocated for the causes she represented, it is unlikely that members of the communities she collected from, including the American Indian Movement and the Social Human Rights Party, ever considered her a member (Message 2014: 78–79). She recognized the distrust many activists felt toward the Smithsonian Institution and other museums and federal government agencies, and rapport was her key technique for gaining access to the communities producing the materials she wanted to collect. Despite being progressive in the 1970s, Mayo's actions would likely attract this kind of response if adopted today:

> … it's all well and good for the Smithsonian and New York Historical Society, who I respect, to sort of swoop in and cherry pick some items to get them in their collections representing the movement so that in seven years time they can put on an exhibit and sort of try to turn it into a museum curiosity instead of what the sense I got from the working group was of ownership of the story and you see that particularly with underrepresented communities, whether it's with you know, racial or ethnic minorities, or you know socially and economically disadvantaged communities who don't have a stake in documenting how it got and how it is presented. And that's the sense I got from the working group: why the people who participated in it, felt it was important because outside institutions were coming in and they weren't staying and I don't know, how much were they talking to or listening to people who were very much deep in the movement.
>
> (See Roberts n.d.h: 12)

The distinction between insiders and outsiders also remained in place throughout Occupy, where participants were required to declare any conflicts of interest.[10] Inhabiting a position similar to Mayo were Tamiment Library staff members who, despite the inclusive remit of the Archives Working Group, were designated as advisers rather than insiders by core working group members. Even Michael Nash, director of Tamiment Library, who had been a regular presence until his death and whose contribution was valued by the group, was considered an outsider (see Roberts n.d.h: 12).

Parallels also exist in the way the collections made by Mayo and the Occupy Wall Street Archives Working Group were received by participants in the movements from which they collected. For example, the argument that Occupy should not be collected because 'This movement is still happening; it's not history yet' (Roberts n.d.i; also see Roberts n.d.h: 17) uncannily evokes allegations made by conservative historian and director of the Smithsonian National Museum of History and Technology, Daniel Boorstin, and others. According to Boorstin, contemporary collecting was 'presentist', 'biased', and lacking in judicious and energetic historical perspective … [demonstrating a] preoccupation with confrontation politics' (Boorstin quoted in Message 2014: 84, 90). While Occupy's 'leadership' (in the form of the General Assembly) voiced suspicion of the archives on the grounds that the movement should focus on its future, not its past, Boorstin's argument was based on criticism that contemporary collecting implied a lack of intellectual distance from the event that was being collected (Message 2014: 85).[11] On one occasion, he issued a warning about the dangers of confusing 'journalistic topicality with historical relevance'. The issue of 'presentism' and the benefits and challenges of contemporary collecting (from everyday life generally as well as in response to specific events) were widely debated across the museological profession. A 1974 article in a professional magazine, *Museum News*, called 'The Past Is Prologue' asks '[W]ould your museum allow a curator to attend rallies and protest demonstrations or to meet with activists of various persuasions in pursuit of contemporary materials?' (quoted in Message 2014: 80). Despite 40 years of separation, the problematic politics of insider/outsider status and identifications today remain current.

The historical context for contemporary collecting can be explored further through a survey conducted in 1983 by a working group at the National Museum of American History, which was called the '20th Century Collecting Committee' (Message 2014: 85–86). The survey was sent to around 100 museums, local historical societies and other relevant places (including the Library of Congress) to participate in what was called the '20th Century Project'. Curators were asked to evaluate current practices (their own and that of others), to comment on whether their museums had formal policies in place, and to describe what challenges they saw as being affiliated with or caused by the practice of collecting twentieth-century materials. They were asked to focus particularly on contemporary ephemeral objects which are easily lost or destroyed, and which therefore would require a conscious preservation effort while still plentiful and inexpensive. Although this group of mainstream curators based at established (although sometimes small) museums was asked to respond to collecting contemporary materials generally (not just cause-based), analogies exist in the 25 detailed responses received and the responses attracted by a remarkably similar set of questions asked 30 years later by Amy Roberts of a small group of professionally trained archivist members of the Occupy Wall Street Archives Working Group. For example, a response typically voiced in reply to the 1983 questionnaire was 'I am on the pro side of the controversy concerning collecting contemporary materials. ... Who better than ourselves can or should say what we are about?'[12] Responses to questions about how to collect and assess the value of contemporary culture were also remarkably similar, with ideas of open calls and 'scavenger hunts' suggested by participants of both Roberts' questionnaire and the earlier survey alike (Message 2014: 86; also see Roberts n.d.h: 12).[13]

The questions asked by Roberts of the much smaller set of activist archivists included:

- What were you collecting and where did you keep it?
- Do you think it was necessary for Occupy to document itself? Do you think it was necessary for there to be a working group?
- What role do you think archives and memory can have in social movements?
- What role do you think the archives project played in the Occupy Wall Street Movement?
- Did you feel that there was a division within the Archives Working Group membership between its archivists and activists?
- What did you think were the biggest challenges and limitations faced by the working group in realizing its mission? How do you think these challenges are similar to or different from challenges faced by other archival collections?
- Did you want to comment on what factors you think influenced discourse in the working group?
- What do you think about the decision to donate the OWS Archives to the Tamiment Library and Archives?
- There seemed to be a fair number of misunderstandings between the working group and others in the Occupy movement about archival terminology and concepts. Please describe what these mean to you in relation to archives.[14]

Roberts' questionnaire also included an invitation for respondents to reflect on what they, either as individuals or collectively as a working group, might have done differently. She also sought recommendations on what respondents would advise others who might seek to create archival collections for contemporary social movements. The responses demonstrate a clear connection with previous instances of curatorial and archival activism. They also provide first-person accounts of the perspectives taken by individual activist collectors, and reflection on decisions made by the group.[15] The questionnaire exists as a primary source for attempts to understand the archive, making its questions, and the material and conceptual answers they yielded, factors that need to be considered in any attempt to conduct a collections-based analysis of its contents, which is an exercise I model in Chapter 2.

Activist archiving

The Archives Working Group was committed to activist archiving. At its most general, this term refers to the actions of archivists who can be self-identified rather than professionally credentialed or qualified who wish to pursue, advocate for, and reflect a social justice agenda that is usually specific to a particular cause. Activist archiving is often related to community archiving (Erde 2014). It is often perceived to be a form of counter-practice antagonistic to government and private (corporate) institutional archives. The dichotomy between community-generated interests and institutional agendas has arisen for various reasons, including issues around resources and access. Community archives may have less access to professional conventions, resources, and expertise, while larger institutions may have fewer pathways for accessing communities and individuals whose work and lives are represented by the archives they produce. While community archives may be more committed to the principle of being inviting and accessible to the community in which they are embedded, logistical issues can mean that in reality they become less open and inclusive of users than larger counterparts with greater resources.

Drawing instrumental oppositions comes, however, at the cost of understanding the potential for activist archives and organizations to work with and across community, government, and other organizational spheres. For example, while community-based archives have been characterized as less professional and more subjective than institutional archives, Randall C. Jimerson is not alone in believing that 'self-documentation and even partisanship may be necessary to ensure preservation [and I would add here appropriate treatment] of culturally sensitive or confidential information [and materials]' (Jimerson 2013: 339). Further, despite asserting the agency, authority and specific demands of community identities, defining 'community' as a cohort that exists (always already, somehow constitutionally) in opposition to and independent of mainstream institutions risks missing opportunities to force discussions about the exclusion of certain communities from mainstream or homogenous archival representations. In so doing, it risks underplaying the political reach sought by activist (and/or community) archives and the opportunity to create a political intervention into the formative historical and political infrastructure – and national narratives – that mainstream archives reproduce (including those affiliated with governments, universities, and other corporate and professional organizations).

Static definitions also fail to adequately account for interest by 'mainstream' institutional archivists in the practice of activist archiving. There is increasing interest by professionally employed archivists in exploring what the impact of activism can have on what they do as well as the structure in which they work, in order to influence the narratives they represent. This trend is evidenced by the critical mass of professionally trained archivists who undertook key roles in the Occupy Wall Street Archives Working

Group.[16] In a statement that is consistent with observations made by working group members (for example, see Roberts n.d.h: 35), Michelle Caswell explains the challenges for institutionally based archivists who seek activist engagement on behalf of the records they produce:

> Archivists, like any other bureaucrats in a system, bear responsibility for, and complicity in, the overarching end goal of the system. ... In this way, we are not 'referees' but 'contestants' in the game of history. As contestants, archivists must fully own up to their roles in knowledge production, and critically engage with the ultimate aims of such knowledge. Are we going to carry on with business as usual ...?
>
> (Caswell 2010: 23–24)

Understanding the role of individual archivists and the process-oriented bureaucracies they partake in – be they independent or institutional – as a component of infrastructure building suggests that instead of seeking an encompassing definition of what 'activist archiving' *is*, we might focus on asking what it *does*. This emphasis on action is appropriate to the intention of the Occupy Wall Street Archives Working Group, and recognizes the challenges it faced. Members routinely articulated the difficulties of working across activist and archiving sectors, which included challenges in constructing an archive as an external representation of Occupy Wall Street, from the perspective of an insider. One working member explains:

> The working group placed archivists in an embedded role alongside organizers of the events. This necessarily challenged the neutrality by which an archivist might try to operate in collecting, preserving and organizing collections from past events. A unique challenge was to document the events as they were in progress while assuming that archivists were also influencing the construction of the events as they happened.
>
> (See Roberts n.d.h: 17)

The Occupy Archive offers an example of what resistance by archivists can look like (Chapter 3; Greene 2013: 305). It is built from and demonstrates approaches that create and investigate discussion about how independent organizations, infrastructures, community agendas and practices of mainstream collecting institutions and archives interact, correspond, and differ from each other. There is no single model for activist archiving, which embraces heterogeneity of practice. For example, members of Interference Archive, a cognate organization that had some members in common with the Occupy Archives Working Group, acknowledge that some of the characteristics of their repository are also common to community archives.

These include the provision of local, autonomous spaces that seek to collectivize knowledge production by the representation and preservation of alternative historical narratives and cultural identities. Despite these shared features, Interference Archive claims an explicit distinction from community archives. This difference arises primarily out of intention: Their specific political agenda is to create a prefigurative model that challenges master narratives and demonstrates the limitations of accepted practice and knowledge often employed in historical archives (both large-scale institutional and small-scale community organizations) that focus on outcomes rather than process. Members of Interference Archive have expressed the view that:

> Activist archives not only honor specific communities but also forge new relationships between parallel histories, reshape and reinterpret dominant narratives, and challenge conceptions of the archive itself. … [t]he activist archive serves as a platform for archivists – as activists – to contribute to the ongoing production of social movements with which they identify.
>
> (Sellie *et al.* 2015: 454)

The interdisciplinary exchange that is required to forge new relationships across traditions and practices means that activist archives can show archives and social reform movements as being both socially and subjectively constructed and experienced. Created through, and as a material record of, the interactions between individuals and groups, as well as organizations and institutions, archives and social movements attribute significant value to the roles played by history and narrative in the production of collective meaning. Both recognize that history and narrative are highly contested instruments. Activist archivists often aim to undermine the taken-for-granted authority of certain narratives (around nation and nationalism for instance), which are often presented in the public sphere as inalienable end products. One strategy they employ is to use a first-person perspective to explore the diverse life histories of a collection, its materials, its producers, and users, and the places in which it has been construed with meaning. They do this to emphasize that personal narratives can 'draw attention to embodied activist experience and to heterogeneity of activist interpretation', thereby 'making visible the fragile and contested character of more collective stories' (Eschle 2018: 528).

Writing lives through things

The Occupy Archive is a material-based record of Occupy Wall Street. It was produced by participants according to a mission and collection development plan that sought to highlight the contribution that material and documentary culture can offer to understandings of human action and society. The collection was produced through processes of autoethnography (as a method of data gathering) and life writing to communicate first-person lived experience through forms of expression that describe, analyze, or critique cultural, political, and social meanings and understandings, and the relationships between individuals or groups and larger social structures (Maréchal 2010). The Archives Working Group sought to collect

> as much movement-related material as possible: cardboard signs, posters, flyers, manifestos, zines, documents by working groups, and all manners of digital media. At present, OWS Archives has collected thousands of discrete pieces, and that count grows daily. At present, the main storage locations are dedicated OWS spaces – SIS (Shipping, Inventory, Storage), and the Occupied Office.
>
> (Questionnaire n.d.)

In addition to proto-institutional records, organizational documents, and objects transferred from storage units to private homes and eventually into the Tamiment Library, the archive includes personal narratives, diaries, and some other editorial modes of expression associated with life histories (oral histories). The archive exists as a data-set that represents a collective life story of the movement.

Autoethnography and life writing approaches are compatible with the working group's project of representing people and context through objects. They share an interest in developing narratives by and about the self to assert individual empowerment and agency in the name of collective action. Autoethnography and life writing can be used to make apparent the links between an individual participant narrator and the social, political, organizational, and other systems that produce the environment that is being experienced and recorded. Acknowledging the role of life writing, Eschle argues that 'movements like Occupy *are*, in large part, the stories their participants (as well as their opponents and wider publics) tell about them' (Eschle 2018: 527). Central to this task, though, is understanding relationships between participants and material culture, and part of the reason that autoethnography and life writing provide appropriate methods for collections development and analysis is because they each emphasize 'the kind of understanding that consists in seeing connections' (Wittgenstein quoted in Monk 2007: 527).[17] Indeed, as my previous discussion has shown, archives, from informal organizations through to the most regulated institutional forms of infrastructure, are all about associations.

Rather than existing as a discrete commemoration of a past event to be relegated to the dustbin of history, the collection was understood by members of the Archives Working Group as a 'living resource' that could shape and influence the views of constituents (within and outside of the movement). It was created to challenge traditional forms of institutional power by modeling an alternative approach to activist archiving that privileged collaboration and relationship building (Bold 2012b). The approach taken to collection development emphasized the importance of the embeddedness of archivists in the research process and their interactions and associations with other stakeholders (both internal and external to the movement). It focused on the materiality of the records collected, the technologies and structures of the movement, and articulating how its practices challenged the conventions of broader institutional professions.[18] Autoethnography, which Ellis, Adams, and Bochner (2010: n.p.) describe as 'both process and product' is an appropriate description for how the working group undertook this work. Other scholars also highlight proximity as a key characteristic of autoethnography. Adams, Holman Jones, and Ellis (2015: 2) present it as a research method that shows 'people in the process of figuring out what to do, how to live, and the meaning of their struggles'. The focus on experience and exploring different ways of doing things means that autoethnographic narratives often aim to engage their audiences in political issues (Chang 2008). These characteristics mean that an autoethnographic approach can be a tool that is well suited for activism and activist expression.

Life writing similarly provides first-hand stories and accounts of individuals and their relationship with society, history, organizational infrastructure, and public and political life. It examines the civic lives and duties of objects and institutions as well as the experiences of individuals, families, and groups. It is often associated with ethnographic or autoethnographic methods because one of the principal things ethnographers do, according to James Clifford (1986: 2, 6), is writing: 'the making of texts'. In addition to their own writing and recording of events, a principal undertaking of the Archives Working Group was the collection of 'texts' that had been produced throughout the life cycle of Occupy Wall Street. Letters, diaries, journals (written and documentary), anthropological data, oral testimony, eye-witness accounts, organizational materials such as meeting agendas and notes, and a wide range of other object-based material evidence were all collected. The working group's approach emphasized their own personal and collective experiences of the movement, as well as the working group's role within the prefigurative, proto-organizational structures of Occupy Wall Street. Their intentions are clearly articulated in the group's mission statement:

> Occupy Wall Street Archives Working Group is a collecting initiative, which preserves, safeguards, and makes accessible the records of OWS. It is the repository of the legacy that we will leave for the

future generations. Occupy Wall Street Archives Working Group collects ephemera, signs, posters, audiovisual materials, digital files, photographs, oral histories, and artifacts. It stands as evidence of how participatory democracy can work, how culture and politics connect, and how the 99% can come together to generate social and economic change. Occupy Wall Street Archives Working Group also documents the decision making processes of OWS, of the General Assembly, Coordinators, Think Tank, and Occupiers' meetings, as well as the records of the other subgroups.

(Roberts 2011a)

In practical terms, the Occupy Archive itself stands as a collective life story of a movement dedicated to the diverse demands of 'the 99%'. It also provides an account of the life cycle of the Occupy Archives Working group, from its establishment through to its informal ending.

Autoethnographic collecting

The Archives Working Group's methodology for collecting was determined less by a specific theoretical framework, formal criteria, protocols, or professional standards than it was by circumstance and opportunity. Decisions about collecting often needed to be made spontaneously by individuals rather than through consensus. Collecting decisions were also affected by challenges to accessing storage sites (such as the Sanitation area of the camp), and by personal limitations including what could be physically collected and carried at any given time. This embedded experience of collecting can be contrasted with the approach represented by Mayo's curatorial activism, which was motivated not by first-hand participation in an event but by an object list that she created in advance of selecting or attending a protest to target for the desired materials.[19] In at least one case, Mayo maintained a 'dream list' of materials she aimed to source to represent the lineage between historical and contemporary American Indian protest and reform movements (Message 2014: 112). For her, narrative preceded materiality, whereas the opposite was true for the Archives Working Group. However, discussion of Mayo's activism continues to be relevant for understanding the actions undertaken by the Archives Working Group and the challenges they faced.

A committed feminist, Mayo was certainly an advocate for social justice causes (Message 2014: 82). Her account of the challenges of curatorial activism designed to expand the scope of representation in the National Museum of American History is particularly instructive when she describes the approaches she took to including materials from movements with which

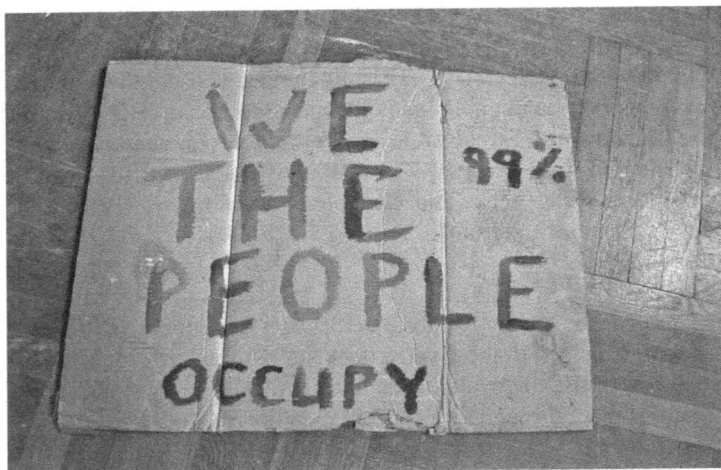

Figure 1.2 'WE THE PEOPLE OCCUPY' protest sign from Occupy Wall Street. Unknown creator. Image from Amy Roberts' private collection (acquired by Tamiment Library in 2017).

Photograph by Kylie Message.

she was not directly aligned. She (and Keith Melder) also had close personal relationships with communities and individuals within the African American civil rights movement (Message 2014: 78), and over her career she built connections, albeit formal ones, with members of the American Indian Movement. However, one example of collecting outside of her personal network included documentation of the election of the Social Human Rights Party in Ann Arbor, Michigan, in 1972 – an event that was nationally significant for demonstrating the impact of reducing the voting age. Two members of the Social Human Rights Party, Gerald De Grieck and Nancy Weschler had gained upset wins in their local areas, stunning the city and gaining nation-wide media coverage. They declined Mayo's requests to provide materials, and when items from their campaign were displayed in the *We The People* exhibition in 1975, sometime after the exhibition had opened, a journalist interviewed De Grieck, who said that the museum 'must have got it [the information] from the FBI'. He questioned if the Smithsonian really understood the politics behind the Social Human Rights Party before it put up the display. Weschler described the Smithsonian's interest in the SHRP's 1972 victories as 'strange' (Message 2014: 79).

The collecting style used by Mayo to obtain materials has a contemporary equivalent, which members of the Archives Working Group referred to as 'guerrilla' collecting (see Roberts n.d.h: 12). An alternative description would be 'helicopter' collecting, whereby a representative from an external institution descends, obtains materials, and returns to their establishment (Sellie *et al.* 2015: 456).[20] Although the National Museum of American History did not have a policy determining principles or protocols for contemporary cause-based collecting until the 1980s, Mayo's dream list of American Indian activist materials generally accepted professional museological criteria for assessing 'collectability' or value based on the items demonstrating one or more of the characteristics of being rare or unique; representative or typical (of a particular type of thing or event); part of a set; or cheap and accessible (Message 2014: 84–85; also see Gardner 2015 on collection planning).

While also not having a formal collecting 'policy' or plan per se, these criteria were also employed as a default mechanism by the Occupy archivists, whose resulting collection shows that choices were made to represent uniqueness of form; uniqueness of information; uniqueness of a process that is shown; or uniqueness of aggregation (that the item is part of a set that is more than a sum of its parts) (Roberts n.d.e). This approach was confirmed by Roberts, who said that in attempting to develop a general framework to work within, the Archives Working Group remained mindful of the 'Criteria that institutions use to determine what to prioritize for $$: 1. Uniqueness, 2. Affordability, 3. Users, 4. appropriate to mission, 5. "sexy", 6. Format' (Roberts n.d.d). Reliance on this criteria in the absence of any other came about partly as a result of the fact that despite working outside of (and in opposition to) an established institutional setting, many participants of the Archives Working Group were trained archivists concerned with the intellectual as well as pragmatic challenges of the work they were doing. Many of the questions raised in the Smithsonian's '20th Century Collecting' project survey and working group from 1983 were also registered as issues or challenges for the Occupy Wall Street Archives Working Group. These included questions about 'what types of media and ephemera and materials do you think are most important to be made available and saved for the long term? ... How can the archive be as accessible as possible. ... What to do with materials made out of cardboard – preservation' (Roberts n.d.d).

The group's work did not substantively progress from collecting through to a processing phase, which includes appraising and describing records (despite one member's nascent interest in developing cataloging methodologies).[21] However, preservation was a constant concern for members of the Archives Working Group, who did not have access to the institutional resources or support enjoyed by most of the respondents to the Smithsonian's earlier survey. In addition, the Occupy Wall Street Archives Working Group faced problems that could not have been imagined by respondents to the earlier survey. Challenges included 'crumbling and falling apart posters'; extreme mold; how to transport items to keep as flat as possible (use Plexiglass to flatten warped sign); how to isolate unstable signs that would affect others; more mold; running paint; how to photograph each sign before and after treatment that equated to a basic form of triage to remove excess debris such as pizza and other food remains – 'Anything stuck to it that can be removed without damaging object' (Roberts n.d.k). Adding to the difficulties of field- and participant-based activist collecting was the ever-present risk of personal injury:

> the archivists who will ultimately process the collection at Tamiment will be paid to do it, and they won't have to worry about arrest, or being punched by a cop while they're working in it – they also won't have to worry about keeping the material out of the rain or safe from tourists who want to 'take that really cool sign home as a souvenir'.
>
> (See Roberts n.d.h: 18)

Although a majority of respondents to the Smithsonian's 1983 survey identified as activist curators or archivists at mainstream institutions (of varying size and scale), most expressed uncertainty about how to assess the long term value of ubiquitous contemporary items. In contrast, members of the Occupy Wall Street Archives Working Group were much more comfortable with the idea of 'making a value judgment about what is worth saving' (Roberts n.d.e, *emphasis in original*). They placed less emphasis on keeping things 'forever' than on the idea of preserving a sense of their 'useful life' and 'enduring value' … in other words, they generally supported the idea of keeping things as long as they're useful [tell us something meaningful] or valuable (Roberts n.d.e).[22] One record of notes from February 2012 indicates key concerns of the Occupy Wall Street Archives Working Group as being:

- Custodianship
- Selection and triage
- Preservation; not everything needs to be kept
- Uniqueness of process
- Uniqueness of information
- Grouping of materials that as individual items don't mean anything

(Roberts n.d.e)

The suspicions expressed by the Social Human Rights Party (and from time to time, other activist organizations and members) about the Smithsonian's intentions for collecting their reform materials echo many of the concerns articulated by the Archives Working Group about the prospect of a formal association with established institutions. These concerns were exemplified in the negotiation between the Archives Working Group and Tamiment Library, but they also influenced opinions about other institutions that had a (usually passing) presence on site. The Archives Working Group sought to protect the independence of the archive and was insistent on remaining separate from any other outside institutions that were collecting material. Asked by a journalist's questionnaire at one time if 'occupiers see it as a contradiction of the spirit of the movement that so-called establishment institutions (Smithsonian, etc.) are actively collecting materials?' they responded: 'Occupiers understand that so-called establishment institutions, such as Smithsonian, are actively collecting materials; all we can do, from within the movement, is collect as much as possible and act as our own stewards of our shared history.' In response to the journalist's question, 'Has there been competition among institutions vying for certain Occupy materials that you are aware of? If so, what do you make of that?' they said they had not been approached by very many institutions. The Smithsonian had not approached the Archives Working Group. 'Many institutions', they responded, 'have taken an interest and have collected material but very few have approached us about the materials that we have or that they should be collecting' (Questionnaire n.d.). One working group member addressed the lack of collaboration in the following way:

> Archives traditionally wait for the records to come to them. Archivists have an obligation to fill in the historical gaps. The sense that I got was that most archivists were not investing time and were doing guerilla attempts to obtain items and then taking them back to where they were working which is not wrong, but in the context of OWS, from my perspective, it would have been nice to see a little bit more organized professional support with the movement.
>
> (See Roberts n.d.h: 12)

In the end, fatigue and the realities of maintaining an archive unsupported by the movement and isolated from professional resources took its toll on the working group. Roberts wrote 'Can't break your back and heart trying to preserve and organize your collection. Resources are limited and [you] do the best you can' (Roberts n.d.e).[23]

A material data-set

Material culture is a relational and critical category. The materiality of the Occupy Archive is fundamental to the story it tells. The collection's materiality, sensory experience and embodiment evidence conflict and negotiation as components of a social movement. Material elements are also central to the associations and networks the collection builds, and the transactions and exchanges it represents. They present meaning in a way that words cannot always achieve, and in a way that leads us 'to reflect on object-subject relations in a manner that has a direct bearing on our understanding of the nature of the human condition and social Being in the world' (Tilley 2011). The abundance and diversity of things (such as banners and signs) within the collection also contributes to 'the universe of signs' that is commonly attributed to protests (Mitchell 2013a; Mitchell 2013b; Taussig 2013). The collection presents a physical – material – articulation of the multiplicity of demands and views that would be otherwise impossible to capture *en masse* or generalize. Indeed, this multiplicity was key to the movement's insistent rejection of demands that it provide a single demand to represent the complaints of the 99%.

Materiality can also usefully contribute to and complicate modes of representation typically associated with ethnographic collection methods and life-writing narratives. The autoethnographic approach taken to produce this collection 'grounds' the universe of signs that are easily commoditized both within institutional settings or the world at large. The first-person approach to collection development shifts the referent from being an indexical one to a pragmatic one so that objects can be understood as having meanings that are multiple, relational, and shifting, rather than inherent or unchanging (Pearce 2010: xviii). The haptic nature of the material records guided decisions made by the collection's creators. It also provokes the researcher in the archive, whose experience of working through files, objects, documents, databases, and so on, is materialized by engagement with the papers and things at their fingertips. While Taussig's (2013) and Mitchell's (2013b) accounts of Occupy Wall Street provide evocative accounts that focus on the crowds of bodies holding placards at Liberty Plaza, I suggest that the Occupy Archive provides another angle to the story that can be understood as a collective and embodied narrative of the experience as told through its material products and residue: a form of writing movement lives through things.

The materiality of objects, including waterlogged papers, ripped signs and personalized UPS delivery stickers, play a part in the field of knowledge about Occupy that includes but is not exhaustively contained within this collection. The experience of being witness to the events of Occupy is represented not by the crowds, bodies, or faces described by Taussig (2013) or Mitchell (2013b), but by the often rapidly produced and ubiquitously dirty materials that are a defining characteristic of this assemblage. In the final instance, the Occupy Archive reflects the process of activism, the activity of contemporary collecting, and an attempt to simultaneously document these processes. Balancing these three tasks was far from easy for the group of individuals who were making up 'the rules' (of activist archiving for Occupy) as they went along. Minutes from one meeting of the Archives Working Group held during the Zuccotti Park occupation in which an upcoming action was being organized indicates the difficulty that arose for working group members who had to juggle the responsibilities that came with being activists and archivists:

> Time's Up / Critical Mass meetings at Canal at 6:00 am. … Police Spotter and crowd liaison … Requires a lot of organization and timing … Archives – collect people's signs from C/# – this will be a challenge.
> (Roberts n.d.g)

The personal is political

The Occupy Archive brings together individual and collective narratives and explains some of the conflicts that arose for people who identified as both activists and archivists. It insists on recognizing the collective experience and personal impacts of the movement on the people who associated with or made Liberty Plaza their home. An alternative approach to collection development might have found swooping up the detritus of the occupation to be adequate, but the Archives Working Group did not want to just collate 'the stuff' of Occupy. They sought explicitly to document the political and anti-institutional processes of the movement from the perspective of occupiers, and to represent the role that materials such as protest banners and signs, as well as meeting agendas and minutes, made to the development of the movement as a political exercise. As such, their techniques required embedded and embodied collecting. They targeted materials that reflected the movement's processes as well as internal planning, decision-making, regulations, and policies where they existed. While it was impossible to capture the authorship for most of the individual materials included in this assemblage, the collection demonstrates that the 99% occupying Wall Street championed a multiplicity of demands, views, and causes. The group's commitment to representing the movement fully is evident in their inclusive and self-conscious approach to collecting, as Roberts recorded in one notebook entry:

> The next challenge for the archives is making sure that more of the movement is represented. There are absences in institutional archives but there can also be absences in a movement archive. … The occupation created a commons where people could come together and learn about anything they wanted to learn and could also resist, reclaim, and recreate. I think the raid that happened on November 15 shows the

importance of archiving a movement like Occupy Wall Street as it happens because so much of what was generated physically was destroyed. ... I had to collect the signs that I thought were weird and had messages that I didn't politically agree with such as End the Fed which was a pretty common theme in some of the signs. I'm an anti-capitalist and don't think ending the Fed is the answer to the economic crisis but I can't ignore the sign just because I don't agree with it. So that is an example of how being a participant can bias you a little.

(Roberts n.d.i)

Also included in the notebooks from time to time – usually in the margins – is a private and self-reflective narrative in which Roberts questions her personal role, intentions, and responses to events, decisions, and activities. The reflections demonstrate the connections that exist between individual identity, the effect of internal and interpersonal relationships and group dynamics, and the impact of institutional politics beyond the Archives Working Group in context of the wider movement. Although this is not specifically Roberts' archive or narrative, I have included these details to recognize the voice of the archivist.[24] I also want to show that the notebooks and the collection to which they now contribute demonstrates the working group's levels of self-awareness regarding the collections development process. For example, in one notebook, Roberts addresses what she calls a 'personal' challenge: 'Started to realize in the course of archiving the movement that it's impossible to have an objective or balanced view of history and it's impossible to have a balanced archive. There is always a bias that is reflected in who collects the materials for the archive' (Roberts n.d.d). Looking closely at these notebooks, which transgress the boundaries between the personal and the political, can facilitate understanding what Stoler means when she advocates for recognizing the archive as a subject rather than as an objective source (Stoler 2002: 87–109). Furthermore, in terms of collections analysis and broader collection development frameworks, understanding the relationship of the collection to its creators and the community within which the collection occurred is critical because this context directly influences how traditional concepts such as 'value' need to be adjusted and applied to contemporary cause-based collections.

The notebooks were not intended to be private diaries. They reveal much more about the urgent daily actions and operations of Occupy during the occupation as well as into the post-occupation period of 2012 than they do about personal interactions.[25] It is difficult to map the same names across the entire period covered by the collection.[26] While two or three (maybe four) people are mentioned across the whole period covered by the collection, the notebooks reflect three phases of involvement by roughly three cohorts of core Archives Working Group members, who move into and out of the note-book's narratives in roughly chronological order. The demographics of the Archives Working Group was similar to that of the Library Working Group, about which Zachary Loeb, who was a member of both (and employed as a librarian at New York Public Library), explained:

> The demographic of OWSL [Occupy Wall Street Library] members was varied, consisting of full-time activists, artists, retirees, college profes-sors, poets, students, parents, punks, a wandering Canadian, and profes-sional librarians (with many fitting into several categories at once). About half of the regular librarians were professional librarians or archivists – those with master's degrees, whether employed in the field of not – or in a similarly scholarly profession. Many of the drop-in librarians were also professionals, paraprofessionals, or LIS students; we had visitors from Radical Reference and the Pratt SILS program, among others.
>
> (Taylor and Loeb 2014: 273)

The constituency of the Occupy Wall Street Archives Working Group was similar to that of the Library Working Group, with a high proportion of professionally trained archivists, librarians, and graduate students in related fields. The transient nature of people's involvement was also a condition of all working groups associated with the movement. Problems caused by an inconsistent 'workforce' were commonplace, created by people's com-ings and goings, either as the result of disinterest or disillusionment, or for practical reasons associated with balancing a commitment to the move-ment with their employment, family, long commutes to meetings, and other responsibilities.[27] One member recalled that 'membership was constantly in flux'. With 'thousands of people going through the park', achieving the open consensus required for decision-making was almost impossible (see Roberts n.d.h: 27).

Regardless of barriers, Occupy Wall Street promoted the idea that con-sensus privileges the authority of the group over the opinion of any indi-vidual member (Graeber 2011). The process of achieving consensus was described in the following terms by a member of the Library Working Group who was also a member of the Archives Working Group:

> The Library Working Group works on consensus. ... For us, consensus requires that nearly everyone support a decision. ... Degreed librarians have no more weight in making decisions than an 18-year-old college student, an underemployed actress, or a crusty traveling kid.
>
> (Fagin, Hen, Loeb, Norton and Taylor 2012 conference presentation quoted in Taylor and Loeb 2014: 275)

The Archives Working Group employed a similar strategy to draw attention to multi-vocal decision-making processes over outcomes. It is also evident in the collection. If the collection focused only on recording outcomes all we would know was that consensus had been achieved, yet the record of process tells us how it was negotiated, by whom, and when it broke down.

Broad inclusivity and representation was a priority for the Archives Working Group, and it is a feature of the historical record produced by the collection. Their 2012 application for registration as an Operations Group within the movement explained 'The OWS Archives is not a closed group; we are open to anyone becoming involved and participating in the documentation process' ('Group registration form' n.d.). This view was similarly represented in a budget proposal made at around the same time: 'Anyone who is interested in participating in this [working group] can do so, in the spirit of this movement you do not have to be a professional archivist to work with us' ('OWS Archives Budget Proposal' 2012).[28] Although a diversity of participation was welcomed, the horizontal structure's insistence on democratic inclusion also created challenges: 'How do you build community and respect autonomy whilst under police surveillance and violence? In a context where people did not necessarily know each other, there was interpersonal conflict, as well as conflict over space, and political arguments' (Roberts n.d.g).

In contrast to the broader 'nonpartisan' support expressed for the People's Library,[29] the Archives Working Group and project remained beleaguered by accusations of elitism and irrelevance. These concerns frequently affected their interactions with other participants of the Occupy movement. In a speech delivered to an open forum early in 2012 that sought to attract donations for the collection and placate concerns about the involvement of the privately owned New York University (which owns Tamiment Library), Roberts justified the role of professional archivists in the Archives Working Group on the grounds that they played an intermediary role between the movement and broader institutional cultures. Referring to herself and Bold, she said: 'Please keep in mind that this archive is going to be used by researchers. Jez [Jeremy] and I are participants and supporters in this struggle so we offer the perspective and views [that are] not being represented' (Roberts n.d.l). Concerns about how to bridge archival work and operational activism also feature in the group's internal debates. In minutes from a meeting in 2012, Roberts writes: 'Yates [McKee] says the problem with the movement is that it's too academic. "Are we trying to build a political mass movement or an intellectual movement?"' (Roberts n.d.c; also McKee 2016).

As perhaps a result of the transient and inconsistent caucus of key members, many of whom voiced strong opinions, the Archives Working

Group – like all working groups – suffered from the creation of cliques and internally competing positions. The loudest, most dominant personalities often gained the most attention (see Roberts n.d.h: 17), and gender, race, and class inequalities were endemic. Managing divisions between working groups as well as interpersonal conflict within them was challenging in a leaderless structure. The need for mediation and improved methods for achieving real inclusivity was mentioned across the movement as it became clear that working groups did not always work in a spirit of coalition building.[30] While these factors were certainly part of the daily life of the Archives Working Group,[31] it soon became apparent that a greater challenge and cause of diminishing morale was that they did not have the support of the General Assembly or broader movement. The working group's application to become a direct action Operational Group did not receive the consensus required at the General Assembly on November 9, 2011. The defeat effectively meant they became ineligible to receive funding for their activities (and their budget proposal was rejected at a General Assembly held the following day, November 10).[32]

The situation of the Archives Working Group was completely different than what was experienced by the Library Working Group, which served a current and visible function at the camp and occupied a central location in the Occupy imaginary because of the daily interaction occupiers had with materials. In contrast, the Archives Working Group struggled to convince people who were 'not involved with the core of the working group and didn't understand the role of the archives' of its value (see Roberts n.d.h: 13). Unlike the library, which was widely regarded as a 'public good', explaining what an archive is and why it should have been supported was a challenge for the Archives Working Group. One member of the working group recalls:

I remember being at the table on one cold blustery night, when there was still money, and talking to someone and them asking how do you ask for money when people are hungry, people are in jail, people are in the hospital, and people are homeless. How do you, and again I value that moment because it puts the challenge of archives in really strong terms. ... why should the money go to the archives instead of the PT or Legal department?

(See Roberts n.d.h: 32)

This comment represents just one instance of the constant interplay between internal, interpersonal and institutional politics that the collection stands as evidence for. Every aspect of the collection ties the personal – as attached for example, to Roberts' notebooks, but as also represented by the signs created by unnamed protestors; the interviews, internal correspondence, and statements made by other working party members; and the documentation of exchanges between the Archives Working Group and the New York City General Assembly and other parts of the movement as well as people from Tamiment Library – to the political. This point is repeatedly asserted by members of the Archives Working Group and is consistently evident throughout the material collection. For example, in explaining the difficulty in disentangling the aspirations and ideals held by individuals from the pragmatics of the movement and the competing agendas of various other working groups, one member commented that:

> The archive was also unfortunate to be stuck between the utopian longings of many OWS activists who expressed a general distrust of hierarchical structures at closed institutions (which most archives are), and 'the woebegone reality that at the end of the day that archival material had to go somewhere', compounded by the deep sense of depressed outrage that consumed many OWS activists in the aftermath of the park being raided.
>
> (See Roberts n.d.h: 20)

Records in the Occupy Archive show how the movement's organizational problems coalesced at this point with an internally fractured working group, interpersonal conflicts, and growing distrust and fatigue across and between working groups and the General Assembly. Thousands of pages of meeting notes, action items, planning documents, and proposal drafts, as well as internal emails and correspondence, constitute a veritable anti-institutional autoethnography documenting what happened in the lead up to the police evacuation of the park, as well as what happened afterward. In the opinion of one member, the work of the Archives Working Group 'largely began after OWS had kind of fallen apart (after the park was raided) and thus they were trying to work at the very moment when people were less and less willing to do OWS work' (see Roberts n.d.h: 18). Disagreement was rife within the Archives Working Group about whether there remained any viable options for maintaining the collection's independence. The General Assembly's rejection of their proposals for funding and their application to gain status as an Operational Group combined with a decision by the Teacher's Federation to evict the Shipping, Inventory, and Storage facility before May Day, leading to an acute crisis in the storage of their materials. One member recounted this period in the following way:

> As OWS steadily shook itself to pieces in the aftermath of the raid (with plenty of infighting and declarations of 'it failed because of you

doing x, y, and z') the groups that still had work to do were caught in impossible positions where they still had to take responsibility for physical items (the archive, the library) after most had moved on to yelling at each other in the digital space.

(See Roberts n.d.h: 20)

In the end, the marginalia and moments of private reflection in Roberts' notebooks increase: 'Very very lonely. ... I miss everyone. Where are they? Is it over? ... People go back to their normal lives' (Roberts n.d.a). The articulation of increasing personal isolation likely reflected the alienation and lack of support of the Archives Working Group from the movement, and the movement's dissemination and inability to rebuild momentum for subsequent activities, including Occupy Wall Street anniversaries and Occupy Sandy. At another point, Roberts writes: 'Struggled to keep this working group together – much the same as the rest of the movement' (Roberts n.d.k). In a later interview, another working group member agrees: 'As a group, I just think its indicative of what happened with all of Occupy. There were different factions and it just broke down' (see Roberts n.d.h.: 21). Another member of the group similarly noted: 'once the media was past talking about them then the park goes away and the media disappears, and the infighting and everything sort of petered out from there. Then nobody wants to archive it anymore!' (see Roberts n.d.h: 13).

At the point the notebooks finish (mid- to late 2012 for the most, although the Occupy Archive includes materials produced and collected into 2013), there was still no resolution about a permanent storage facility for the collection. Discussions with Tamiment Library had stalled.[33] Occupy's trajectory as it is represented in the notebooks and collection more broadly moves from optimism and excitement through to fatigue across the whole movement, to the point where even 'the Documentation working group is not consistently taking notes any more' (Roberts n.d.e), and had 'basically stopped working (on strike!)' (Roberts n.d.e). The materiality of the collection and the wear and tear on it also embodies and charts the progressive exhaustion that affected participants. At the start, new journals were used. Over time, they became dirty, scrunched up, and when full were replaced with notebooks that became water damaged and ripped through the period of police raids. These were replaced by small notepads with increased personal reflections in the margins that were used in the later stages of Occupy through early 2012, when the movement had switched base camp to the freezing cold atrium 60 Wall Street (called 'the real headquarters of OWS' by Gimein 2011) that had palm trees but no heating.

Conclusion

This chapter's account of the intentions and actions of the Archives Working Group has been pieced together from the materials in the archive, and aims to show two things. First, that any social movement is the result of multiple, often competing voices, and that individual agency (even if unnamed) cannot be entirely subsumed by the generalized interests of the movement to which they contribute. Second, this account demonstrates the impossibility of separating or removing personal experience from any archive or museum collection. It seeks to make the point that the story of the group, nation, community, and so on and so forth is also always already personal. The same argument has been made by others, including by members of the Library Working Group:

> The history of the Occupy Wall Street People's Library runs parallel with the history of Occupy Wall Street: it arrived unexpectedly, triggering excitement and interest amongst those who had not anticipated such an occurrence, and now it continues, less visibly, driven largely by those who recognize that resistance is not something you can rely on others to do. You have to do it yourself.
>
> (Taylor and Loeb 2014: 282)

The attention to individual experience and first person narrative that is a feature of autoethnographic collections contrasts with many scholarly attempts to analyze and explore social reform movements. Recognizing the role of individuals in movements and archives, and using the voice of personal experience to represent conflicts, debates, and interactions (rather than as a representation of any singular authority) is something that rarely occurs in social movement studies (Gajdukowa 2002). Indeed, as Broadbent (2018) argues, 'culture has had a hard time finding a full representation in social movement studies' (Broadbent 2018: 749; also Baumgarten *et al.* 2014; Message 2015). The study of political activism has tended to neglect people's personal and social relationships, which were critical to the creation of the Occupy Archive. However, the process of interaction, association building, and transformation does not cease when materials are collected or archived. Narratives retain currency by being recorded in archives and other collections, and continue to exist in physical materials, material wear and tear, as well as discursive, intangible forms. The stories of collections, objects, and the relationships these each cultivate with users 'impart a unique narrative that transforms objects into meaningful artifacts' and continue to exert significance and have a use value even after the event they represent has ended (Humphries and Smith 2014: 490).

Notes

1 I stop short of advocating for the 'anarchives' concept, which was proposed as a decentralized archive of dispersed collections that could reflect 'the nature of social movements as decentralized phenomenon' (#jez3Prez & Atchu 2012).

2 The terminology around the Tamiment collection provides a demonstration of how personal politics and interpersonal bias and conflict can shape what an archive includes and how it is defined. Disagreement within the Archives Working Group about how to define and delineate the collection caused an irredeemable split between individuals who argued for the advantages of Bold's anarchives concept, and those (the broader majority of the Archives Working Group) who did not believe an archive could be decentralized (#jez3Prez & Atchu 2012).

3 Arguments about ownership, donor naming, and provenance are discussed in Evans, Perricci, and Roberts (2014).

4 Despite its significance, the police net remains unprocessed within the collection at Tamiment. It remains held in offsite storage and is not available for public access. Also see Evans, Perricci, and Roberts (2014).

5 The working group was motivated by questions including: 'What affected the functioning of the working group? How can activists ensure access to their own history? And how can history be rewritten depending on who holds power?' (Roberts n.d.d).

6 Logistics and the requirements of training were arduous and filled most days. Scheduling, planning, organizing permits, police spotters, liaison people, and documenting training sessions that included 'de-escalation training for areas where people are staying, AG training, Legal training, People's Wall training' (Roberts n.d.g) make up a large percentage of the internal documentation materials included in the collection, as does training for what to do in the case of arrest:

> Be aware that your actions are going to be filmed; Refrain from screaming at cops; Getting carried while sitting is less painful than going limp and being arrested; If you are sitting down you can choose whether to comply or not; Hand someone your real name and a contact person (should you care).
>
> (Roberts n.d.j)
> Roberts' point here further articulates awareness of the potential
> use of collections material against occupiers, as suggested by
> Besser in (Young 2012)

7 Any attempt at collection analysis will be shaped by the limitations within collections, which are both practical and ideological. Gaps can themselves be recognized as acts of authorship, as Cook explains: 'a major act of determining historical meaning' occurs 'when the archivist fills the box' (Cook 2011: 613). The collection's contents are consistent with this description:

> Although the archive does not contain *everything*, it can amass rather a lot. Diaries, manuscripts, letter, maps, photographs, ledgers, journals, committee minutes, memos, films and objects to name but a few … For the researcher, this volume of 'stuff', that the archive possesses, can be tiresome in nature. There are duplicates and drafts, which are edited and re-edited, memos which circulate, resurfacing in folder after folder.
>
> (McGeachan *et al.* 2012: 171)

8 This person continues:

> Again, without your efforts you all, the collection that now exists at Tamiment wouldn't exist. And that might be an interesting way to look at it in the future ten years from now when the Smithsonian and the New York Historical Society are putting together their exhibits. I think if we took this collection away that's at Tamiment, if it disappeared, what would the historical record look like? Going back to the question about archives. The question does exist. Removing it from the historical record, would it be poorer for it? I would say, yes.
>
> (See Roberts n.d.h: 24)

9 Mayo's approach was more aligned with what we would today call 'guerilla' or 'helicopter' collecting. She says, 'if you are fortunate enough to establish rapport with someone in the group, zero in on the items you want' (quoted in Message 2014: 81).

10 Members were encouraged to declare any institutional affiliations they had, especially if they intended to take advantage of offers of equipment or storage from an institution with which they were connected for the purposes of the Archives Working Group's actions (Bold 2011a; also Schneider 2013b on how he negotiated his potential conflict of interest as a journalist participant of Occupy Wall Street).

11 Allegations of 'presentism' and a perceived lack of 'critical distance' as a negative connotation can be used to defend arguments posed by opposing ends of the political spectrum. The reaction of Tom Fitten (president of Judicial Watch, a conservative watchdog organization) to the Smithsonian's collecting of Occupy is aligned to Boorstin's complaint about Mayo's collecting. 'It looks', said Fitten, 'like it's taxpayer-funded hoarding, as opposed to rigorous historical collecting' (in Salazar and Herschaft 2011; Del Signore 2011). Concerns about how to determine markers for assessing the historical value of contemporary materials and events have also been forward by progressive curators, such as Smithsonian curator Fath Davis Ruffins, who reflected in April 1983 that:

> Part of the problem it seemed to me was that we were trying to come to conclusions when many processes we were examining had not concluded yet. In other words, the 18th century has [by comparison] been over for 183 years. We have generations of historiography about it. There are many conclusive sorts of statements that can be made about it. Neither that body of material nor the critical distance exists when talking about the 20th century. It isn't even *over* yet.
>
> (Ruffins quoted in Message 2014: 85)

12 Robert W. Johnson, curator of American materials at the Children's Museum, Indiana quoted in Message (2014: 86).

13 People within the camp were collecting items, which many will have retained. If the Archives Working Group put out

> a real collecting call in terms of 'the stuff is going to go to this space we're going to donate it', I think some of that stuff would come out of the

woodwork because [people will think] I've got some stuff in my apartment that you guys, I don't want to put it in a storage space because you guys have it in a storage space.

(See Roberts n.d.h: 7)

14 These interviews, conducted by Roberts in the role of researcher rather than collector, contribute a rich resource for further contextualization of the collection. Unfortunately, the interview transcripts that have made their way into the collection are partial, have pages missing, and do not consistently or clearly attribute names to statements. As such, I have anonymized the names of interviewees.

15 The approach taken by Interference Archive to decision making and collections development (which includes a 'preservation through use' policy that does not record user information and does not assess value by longevity of preservation) is described in Sellie *et al.* (2015: 461–63). The significance of Mayo's contribution to post-1970s practices of activist collecting is further acknowledged by Cohen-Stratyner's set of guidelines for collecting from social reform movements' (Cohen-Stratyner 2017: 88–90, referencing Mayo).

16 Whilst there are similarities between this membership and remit and that of other Occupy Wall Street working groups (such as the Library Working Group) and other archives like Interference Archive, the approach of the Archives Working Group can be contrasted with the DIY archiving undertaken in relation to some other collections of activist material, such as the Riot Grrl collection at the Fales Library and Special Collections, also held at New York University (Fales Library and Special Collections 2017; also Keenan and Darms 2013). While these can be described equally accurately as 'activist' collections, the Occupy Archive was created to challenge archival practices and standards as well as the historical narrative that is represented by history. In other words, rather than being a private collection made public, it was designed from the outset to be part of the public register; which is also why the determination for it to be open access was consistently reaffirmed in negotiations with Tamiment Library. Upon transfer of the collection, the conditions governing use of the material in the archive were licensed by the Occupy Wall Street Archives Working Group under a Creative Commons Attribution-Noncommercial 3.0 License (Tamiment Library and Robert F. Wagner Labor Archive 2018; Smith 2011).

17 As Pearce and others have argued, 'culture' also includes and is shaped by the materials and surroundings through which we 'produce the individual and social habits [and networks of relationships] that add up to ongoing life' (Pearce 2010: xvii; Pearce 1994: 25). An interest in material culture focused on 'objects, people and the engagements between them' (Dudley 2010: 1) has been merged with increasing adaptations of Kopytoff's 'biography of an object' approach, which represented objects as culturally constructed entities with social lives. 'What one glimpses through the biographies of both people and things', he argued, 'is, above all, the social system and the collective understandings on which it rests' (Kopytoff 1988: 89).

18 The collection exhibits characteristics that are consistent with anthropological approaches to writing life histories that emphasize the importance of the teller's sociocultural milieu, context, and interpersonal relationships (Reed-Danahay 2011).

19 Mayo's approach to list-directed collecting might arguably increase the likelihood of producing a collection as a '*trace* or *record* of collecting activities and processes' (Star 1999: 387).

20 Over the late 2011 period, the media widely reported 'more than a half-dozen major museums and organizations' as having collected from Occupy. The language used to describe the act of collecting is consistent with a non-systematic or rigorous 'in-and-out' guerilla approach criticized by members of the Archives Working Group. Cristian Salazar and Randy Herschaft (2011) reported, for example, that museums have sent staff 'to rummage' for materials. Shane Ferro reported the 'scooping up' of materials, and quoted an insider who referred to 'grab[bing] material while it's fresh' (Ferro 2011). Following the eviction of Zuccotti Park, the imagery of museums conducting salvage collecting was observed by Allison Kilkenny (2012): 'Occupy is beginning to lose its shininess and the Smithsonian is hurrying after it with a broom and evidence bag'.

21 Cook (2011: 602) articulates the four core archival functions as appraisal and acquisition; arrangement, processing, and description; preservation; and public programming. One member of the Archives Working Group, James Molenda, is reported as having taken on the task of cataloguing artifacts 'as they come in and tagging them, according to theme and medium. "For example", he says, "a cardboard sign protesting police brutality would be dated, tagged with 'police' and 'cardboard' and entered into the catalogue with a low-resolution photograph"' (quoted in Samtani 2011). There is little evidence of practical cataloguing having been actually undertaken in regard to the Tamiment collection, however.

22 This shift reflects broader changes in archival thinking that is evident in the approach taken by other people or institutions collecting from Occupy or commenting on contemporary collecting. Ferro cites historian Kenneth T. Jackson as saying that: [T]he Occupy protests may or may not prove to be a significant movement in the long view of history, but by the time scholars know for sure it will be too late to collect materials. As a museum, he [Jackson] said, 'Your job is not to make the judgment about whether somebody wants to look at it [now] but whether it might be useful to a historian in the future' (quoted in Salazar and Herschaft 2011).

23 All members of the working group recognized practical obstacles and the lack of resources as real problems. 'There was no money, no space', none of

> the things that an archives need. All the things that by definition make an archive an archive. Physical space, supplies, money, really dedicated staff, and even those who among the hardcore working group people you have other jobs, you had other commitments, which is not a negative thing its just reality and trying to create an archives from scratch without the dedicated staff.
>
> (See Roberts n.d.h: 12)

24 Recognizing the agency of the archivist, in this case, of the Occupy Archives Working Group, is important for both the profession and the movement because, as Cook says: 'What is still missing is the voice of the archivist, who, after all, is the principal actor in defining, choosing, and constructing the archive *that remains*, and then in representing and presenting that surviving archival trace to researchers' (Cook 2011: 614).

25 Interpersonal interactions and negotiations about the collection moved into the semi-private online space of a Google group following the occupation's conclusion, primarily because fewer meetings were held.

26 One reason that it is necessary to read across cognate collections (where they exist and can be identified and accessed) is to build a fuller narrative of the event and experience of Occupy because the object-based materials held at Tamiment Library were produced in situ, sometimes urgently, to reflect a current experience or threat. They do not include interpretive material, which can be sourced from other collections, including the private Google group archive of internal working group correspondence that allowed me to more accurately identify participant names and roles. Chapters 1 and 2 of this book focus on the physical object-based materials at Tamiment Library, while the electronic communications from the Google group complement the organizational materials explored in Chapter 3.

27 The realities of people's lives meant that 'all of us were involved on a volunteer basis so time was difficult to schedule meetings ... people didn't have the band-width to do all the work outside of the other work they were doing to live' (see Roberts n.d.h: 17).

28 The full statement in the 'OWS Archives Budget Proposal' (2012) says:

> We are the Archives Working Group. We were created to ensure that Occupy Wall Street preserves and owns its past. We do this by collecting the fliers, signs, posters, audiovisual and digital files and other artifacts that have been generated by this movement. We are also collecting oral histories. There are many institutions collecting these materials, but we think it is necessary that we also archive our own history. We have collected several hundred card-board signs and other materials which are currently in danger of decaying if we do not act now. In order to preserve these for the future we need to take care of them. Right now we have a crisis because we cannot proceed without purchasing certain materials. We meet at 5:00pm on Sundays at 60 Wall St. Anyone who is interested in participating in this can do so, in the spirit of this movement you do not have to be a professional archivist to work with us.

29 About the People's Library, Taussig says three thousand or more library books were lovingly bundled into plastic boxes: 'Together with the poets, the books are the "crown jewels" of this liberated zone, this experiment in "horizontal" decision-making and vertiginous imagination' (Taussig 2013: 20; also see Sacks 2011).

30 Inter-group challenges were widely reported, including in Roberts' notes from one meeting:

> Each AG [Action Group] will do something different – will not work against each other, will not dob each other into police, will support each other... negotiation between them seems complex and competitive (for space and attention as well as GA support and funding).

These agreements had limited success in actuality, where working groups competed for funding, support and attention (Roberts n.d.g). Various issues were raised, including by members of the Facilitation Working Group and Documentation Working Group who were 'tired' of debates over race issues (Roberts n.d.e). Subsequent challenges articulated by the Archives Working Group included: 'How do we build coalitions with other groups? Choosing who we do and don't want to work with; Encampment in the spring; Return to how many GAs per week? And deal with burnout and exhaustion' (Roberts n.d.d).

31   According to one working group member:

> There was still, in the group, this happens amongst us still, and not just with Occupy, there's still the power dynamics of the society that you're in and I don't think that the working group did a very good job of balancing and addressing, figuring out how to not have informal hierarchy power dynamics and that's why you need to have really great facilitation, which I think if we had really skilled facilitators we would have been much better [at].
>
> (See Roberts n.d.h: 19)

32   The rationale for establishing Operational Groups was that:

> Since September 17th Occupy Wall Street (OWS) has grown and inspired occupations around the globe. The General Assembly (GA) is at the heart of this movement. It provides a forum for political discussion and a plurality of ideas. It is, however, struggling to meet the day-to-day operational needs of the Working Groups and Caucuses ... there's more... challenges – access, transparency, participation, functionality, decision-making, accountability, marginalization, time for visioning, trust and solidarity.
>
> (OWS Structure Working Group n.d.)

> Several working groups, including Sanitation and the Library, which had synchronicities with the Archives Working Group and shared several joint members (Dean 2001; Molenda 2011a; Taylor and Loeb 2014), voted against the Archives Working Group's application for registration as an Operational (Direct Action) Group (Dean 2001).

33   The stalling followed the death of Michael Nash. The protraction was likely also related to disagreements over the nature of donor contracts, which may have had more to do with questions about 'who' was required to sign off on the transfer of the collection from 'Occupy' to Tamiment Library than with concerns over protecting the authorship of individual materials (which appeared to have been resolved in a reasonably straightforward manner by allowing materials to be reclaimed at any time by self-identified authors/owners) (Roberts n.d.j).

2 Object lessons
Occupy Wall Street. Bring tent

Collection analysis

Rationale

In the American Fall of 2012, roughly a year after the occupation at Zuccotti Park had taken hold and come to an end, visual studies scholar William J. T. Mitchell reflected:

> The massive outpouring of creativity during this year of crisis, the millions of images conveyed in banners, slogans, videos, photographs, posters, costumes, and performances would seem to render a comprehensive, much less systematic, account impossible. The rapidity and vast archival capacities of digital media render this material hyperaccessible to searching and retrieval, while at the same time it threatens to drown the researcher under a tsunami of material.
>
> (Mitchell 2012: 14)

My rationale for pausing the overarching 'what happened and why' metanarrative of this book to present a collections analysis of a subset of protest signs is influenced by my aim to explore some of the objects that Mitchell refers to as constituting a 'tsunami of material'. I argue that direct engagement with even a small number of the 'millions of images' and artifacts produced out of Occupy Wall Street is a concrete way to counter the overwhelming feeling that any systematic or comprehensive account of the movement is impossible.[1] However, overcoming this impossibility does not require extracting from the collection a singular meaning for the movement it represents. My approach is to advocate for a collection analysis exercise, which is a way to systematically describe and assess a museum, archive, or library collection to produce a synoptic, albeit subjective, overview or summary of the materials. Although it might endeavor to identify patterns or themes, collections analysis work does not have to close down

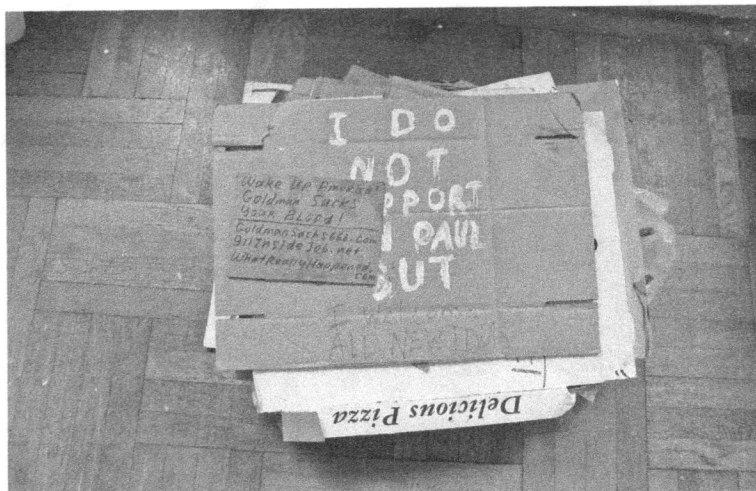

Figure 2.1 Stack of protest signs from Occupy Wall Street. Unknown creators. Image from Amy Roberts' private collection (acquired by Tamiment Library in 2017).

Photograph by Kylie Message.

interpretive possibilities. Starting the analysis task from the premise that the archive is subjective (Atkinson 1992: 354; Stoler 2002) is one way to counter attempts that might seek to reduce the movement to an all-encompassing account. Recognizing the subjectivity of the collection (and researcher) also acknowledges the capacity of the signs to evidence the political intent behind the heterogeneity of demands articulated by the 99%.

While it is important to analyze items individually, this is not an either/ or exercise, because the protest signs were also part of the physical and iconographic universe of Occupy and contributed to the performativity of the movement. The main finding of my collection analysis is recognition of the collection as a group of politically affiliated items that has the authority to speak on behalf of the movement.[2] The agency represented by the signs does not occur because the image of a crowd holding a sea of signs might be more significant from the perspective of indicating a social imaginary than a picture of a single sign, or because there is 'strength in numbers'. Rather, the agency occurs because at the time of their production and use, the signs were intended to form part of a broader field of information. Judith Butler addresses this impact differently, suggesting that even though 'demonstrations and assemblies are often not enough to produce radical change', 'they do alter our perceptions about who the people are, and they assert fundamental freedoms that belong to bodies in their plurality' (Butler 2017). Understanding bodies in plurality and signs in a collection are equally important, as is recognizing the often-collective social activity of sign making and demonstrating for participants of Occupy.

Another reason to spend time describing and thinking about the material culture of the archive is because while Mitchell's comment about the 'hyperaccessibility' of Occupy (Mitchell 2012: 14) might be true for other elements of the movement, widespread digital archiving has not transpired to become a reality for the material contents of the collections created by the Archives Working Group. This should not be taken as a reflection on the 'value' of the collection's content. As Butler (2017) observes, perceptions can be changed even after rallies, movements, and protests draw to a close and people have returned to their 'normal' lives, because the visual record and material residue continue to circulate (in the media, for example) and convey meaning.[3] My response then, to the questions; 'How can one bring into focus both the multiplicity and the unity of this remarkable year? What narrative would be adequate to it?' (Mitchell 2013a: ix–x) is probably unsurprising: *Look at the signs – materially, iconographically and textually, and in context of the collection that they constitute, the communities of practice in which they were produced, and the broader society in which the images circulated.* This response also formed a motivation for writing this book, in which I sought to examine whether a narrative constructed as a result of collections analysis can meet the challenges articulated by Mitchell.

This chapter presents a small part of the analysis that was undertaken for the book. I elected to focus this chapter on analysis of the protest signs as a subset of the Occupy Archive for four reasons. First, the signs have cultural capital because they already hold a place in the public imagination of Occupy Wall Street. Second, the collection was created by the Archives Working Group and reflects the intention for self-representation. Third, despite the tech-savvy nature of the Occupy Wall Street movement, the protest signs were predominantly produced by hand. Fully capturing and conveying their physicality is an important responsibility for the archive. And fourth and finally, the collection has not been catalogued, and remains publicly inaccessible. This material is yet to be digitized as per the discussions determining the conditions of transfer. Although the Occupy Wall Street Archives Working Group's desire for the signs to be re-used by future movements is not ever likely to be realized, I hope the information provided here can contribute to the mission statement of the Archives Working Group, including their intention that the collection: (i) be of some use for future movements in designing actions; (ii) protect the legacy of Occupy as making a contribution to the history of social reform movements and US history; and (iii) represent the movement to future researchers through the materials, voices and perspectives of its participants. 'We want', said one member of the working group, 'researchers to have first-hand accounts of what this movement is, as told by those who are making it happen' (O'Heron quoted in Erde 2014: 25).

Overview

Subject: 125 protest signs collected from Occupy Wall Street, Zuccotti Park. This is a subset of the materials collected by the Occupy Wall Street Archives Working Group, most of which had already been acquired by Tamiment Library. The number 125 is not significant, it just happens to be the number of protest signs that had been stored together (forming a subset of a likely larger collection that had periodically been disseminated at other times).

Collection origin, acquisition, provenance, and context: The signs were produced by participants of the Occupy Wall Street movement. They were collected by members of the Occupy Wall Street Archives Working Group. They were picked up directly from the site or obtained from the Sanitation facility during or soon after the occupation. Although protest signs have become a highly recognized signifier of the Occupy movement as a result of media interest and reproduction, they represent just part of the materials collected by the Archives Working Group. Other materials collected include artwork, buttons, patches, and posters; newspaper clippings and copies of the *Occupied Wall Street Journal*, *Tide*, and other periodicals; personal diaries, fliers, stickers, and postcards; letters of support and Christmas cards; donations of food, clothing, bedding, books, and other supplies addressed from sympathizers sent to Zuccotti Park; organizational documents (meetings agendas, minutes, correspondences, instructions, guidelines, information, etc.); and other three-dimensional ephemera (chains used during direct actions, a donation box used by the Kitchen Working Group, and so on).[4] None of the signs have identified makers (provenance records); only one, possibly two, have marks that might be a signature.

The Occupy Wall Street Archives Working Group Records (Tamiment Library and Robert F. Wagner Labor Archive 2018) reports the content held by the institution as including 75 Linear Feet. 4 boxes of materials are arranged in alphabetical order by type, which accounts only for the publicly accessible (primarily paper-based) materials. (The records note an additional box of electronic records – digital photographs.) The signs and three-dimensional objects are not included in this description. Stored off-site and requiring preservation work, they have not been processed and are not publicly accessible. The protest signs were transferred into the collection in late 2017. I accessed the collection in July 2017 at the private residence where it was being held, not long before it was transferred to Tamiment Library. I documented the collection fully and took photographs of every sign.

Background information (previous storage, preservation, and documentation): In the aftermath of Occupy, the signs were moved around different storage facilities. At the time of documentation in 2017, the signs were being held in storage (in loose piles and plastic bags) in a private home. They have not undergone preservation treatment apart from the urgent *in situ* removal of food, insects, and organic matter such as dirt. Despite some peeling surfaces and paint, as well as some water damage and curled edges resulting from rain during the occupation in which they were created, used, or initially stored, they are in good condition with no signs of damage by moths or other insects, or mold. They had not been previously recorded, either by being digitally photographed, or through any form of text-based cataloguing. The batch of documented materials also included a small number of outlier items, which were excluded from the analysis (10 pages from issues of the *Occupied Wall Street Journal*, one meeting agenda on cardboard, and one FedEx address sticker on the side of a strip of delivery box, which had been retained to show the postal address used for Liberty Plaza).

Description

I coded and classified the signs using basic categories: (1) Materiality, meaning physical form and structure; (2) Presentation, meaning formal characteristics including style of production, visual messaging, and iconography; and (3) Content, including (3a) tone of messaging, and (3b) specific demands. These categories were determined as a result of an initial survey of the signs being analyzed. They reflected my aim to identify shared features and create some general commonalities that would facilitate understanding of any explicit outliers.[5]

1. **Materials.** Physical: Of the total 125 signs, the vast majority, 84 signs, were made from repurposed cardboard boxes; 8 are made from recycled delivery pizza boxes; and 33 signs are made from other materials. Although these are primarily paper-based materials, such as white A4 or A3 paper stuck onto cardboard, paperboard, or white paper-faced foam poster board sheets, the collection also includes one hand-painted/ repurposed plastic bag that looks like it might have originally contained a foam sheet or other flat material. The signs made from repurposed cardboard boxes appears consistent with standard cardboard delivery

boxes or corrugated shipping boxes or mailers, usually uncolored and recycled, most likely square to start with because most of the signs present as square even when they are not pizza boxes. Cardboard boxes were on hand and plentiful at Liberty Plaza, partly because of the extensive quantity of materials being shipped to Occupy from sympathizers throughout the country (as indicated by the FedEx and Amazon delivery labels on some). The boxes were repurposed for a myriad of additional functions, including as mats to sit and sleep on. Other cardboard used for signs includes repurposed waxed fruit and vegetable boxes (marked with crayon) and paperboard drink boxes which are identifiable because of printed brand logos, or from the circle indentations that remain pressed into the surface of the cardboard (made from the weight of holding soda bottles or cans in one of the box's previous lives). Additional structural elements: 3 signs (all double-sided) have handles, of which 2 are made from standard wooden school rulers.

2. **Presentation.** Production (and overall look – home-made or professional): The collection includes 116 handmade signs and 9 printed signs (either by a home printer or mass-produced off-site). Iconography: Image (yes or no): 99 signs feature text-only messages. 26 signs include an illustration or symbol of some kind (all are secondary to

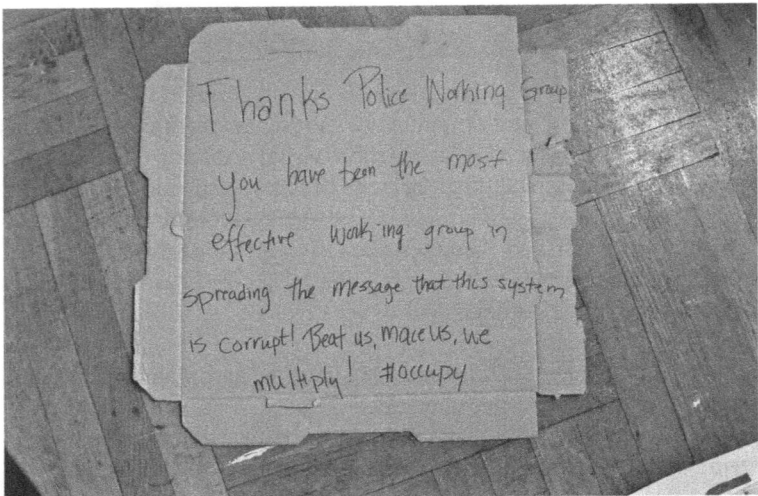

Figure 2.2 Pizza box protest sign from Occupy Wall Street. Unknown creator. Image from Amy Roberts' private collection (acquired by Tamiment Library in 2017).

Photograph by Kylie Message.

the text). There is just one sign that presents an image only (drawn in crayon, probably by a child). Of the signs with images, 21 include color; 5 are black and white. The primary markings of the text-only signs are created with single-color – black or red – permanent marker. There is evidence on many of light pencil markings underneath the marker, indicating the inclusion of a first 'draft' sketch phase. A small number of signs have paint applied roughly with a small paintbrush. The painted signs are more likely to include color. Type style: 98 signs feature capital lettering, either exclusively or dominantly. Close to 100% of signs employ *sans serif* font. Almost all employ exclamation marks, particularly on signs that feature short demands expressed in upper case text. Intertextual (yes or no): 5 signs explicitly integrate written quotations by historical figures (Thomas Jefferson, Martin Luther King Jr, George Washington, Goethe, Gandhi, and Obama). One Obama sign ('Want change? DELIVER IT') parodies the global America image used by his 'Yes we can' campaign logo from 2008. Visual intertextuality is not common (for example, a small number of adaptations, ~3 feature adaptations of the Anarchist symbol). First person (yes or no): 37 signs employ a first-person mode of address. 15 of these refer to an individual 'I', 'me', or 'my' (for example, 'MURDOCH + KOCH OWN THE POLITICAL PROCESS BUT THEY DON'T OWN ME! LOCAL 802'; 'What's the matter? ASK ME'), and 22 refer to a collective 'we', 'us', or 'our'.

3. **Content (3a) Tone of messaging.** The demands were easily accommodated by four tones of expression: Anger and, or exasperation: 62 signs (the majority) include calls for directed forms of action on specific issues like government corruption, police violence, financial inequities, and cause-based phrases such as 'End the Fed', 'bail out ...' 'take back ...'. Statements are negative or focused on redemption or redress ('BOYCOTT FEDERAL ELECTIONS – DELIGITIMIZE THE GOVERNMENT'). Messages in this group sometimes express helplessness or frustration (DESTROY SOCIETY GET $ MILLION$ STAND UP FOR JUSTICE, GET SURROUNDED BY POLICE'). Idealism and/or hope: 51 signs include positive assertions of self-identity, calls for freedom from want (class inequalities, hunger, poverty, education, jobs), freedom from fear (war, peace, broken political and financial systems, and from an environment affected by climate change), or freedom of speech, religion, or humanity ('END RACIAL PROFILING, SUPPORT THE HUMAN Race'). Messages in this category were more likely to feature general phrases of solidarity and community, including 'support ...', 'stand with...', and general statements about voting and democracy ('I WELCOME ALL NEW IDEAS';

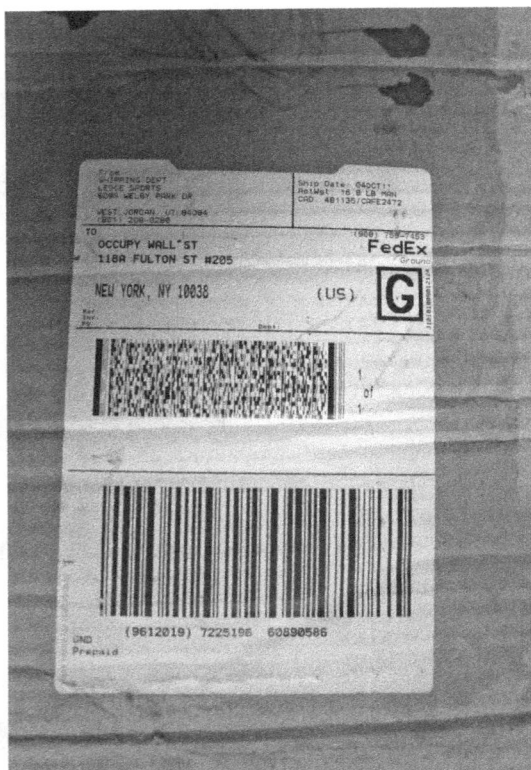

Figure 2.3 Delivery label identifying Occupy Wall Street postal address. Unknown
creator. Image from Amy Roberts' private collection (acquired by
Tamiment Library in 2017).

Photograph by Kylie Message.

'BECOME YOUR DREAM'). Only a very small subset of messages
in this group included specific cause-based calls. Humor: 12 signs
include self-deprecating humor ('I AM A US COLLEGE STUDENT,
Majored in DEBT, Minored in UNEMPLOYMENT!'), absurdity or
irony, sarcasm ('DEAR NYPD, YOUR BEATINGS ONLY MAKE
US STRONGER, LOVE OWS'; 'Thanks Police Working Group. You
have been the most effective working group in spreading the message
that this system is corrupt! Beat us, mace us, we multiply! #occupy'),
or references to parody or pastiche-like forms of culture-jamming.
Interestingly, this collection nowhere references the derivative Guy

Fawkes mask image (would be most likely to appear in this category if anywhere). <u>Language</u>: There is one non-English sign (Spanish) in this group of 125.

3. Content (3b) Specific demands

<u>Political preference</u>: Rather than representing any singular political loyalty, the demands represent the heterogeneity of the movement and the diversity of concerns and ideological leanings articulated by the 99%. Many evidence disillusionment with both 'sides' of politics, as well as the current operational system of capitalism and US democracy. There is a dominant theme of inviting viewers to question basic assumed American ideologies of statehood, nation, and personal identity. Several signs refer ironically to Obama's election-era appeals to the youth vote and calls for change. A small number represent a libertarian or anarchist perspective. Evident in this group of signs is what Jayadev (2011: 28) has usefully called 'the multiple overlapping and sometimes contradictory strands ... from extreme libertarian demands ("End the Fed") to old school socialist credos ("Free School for All"), to more specific grievances ("Destroy the Incarceral State")'. <u>Context</u>: The signs primarily address the national (domestic) context of

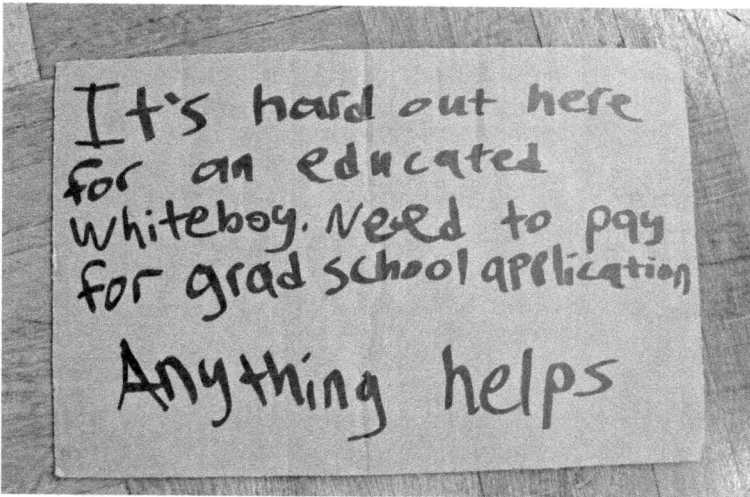

Figure 2.4 Protest sign from Occupy Wall Street. Unknown creator. Image from Amy Roberts' private collection (acquired by Tamiment Library in 2017).

Photograph by Kylie Message.

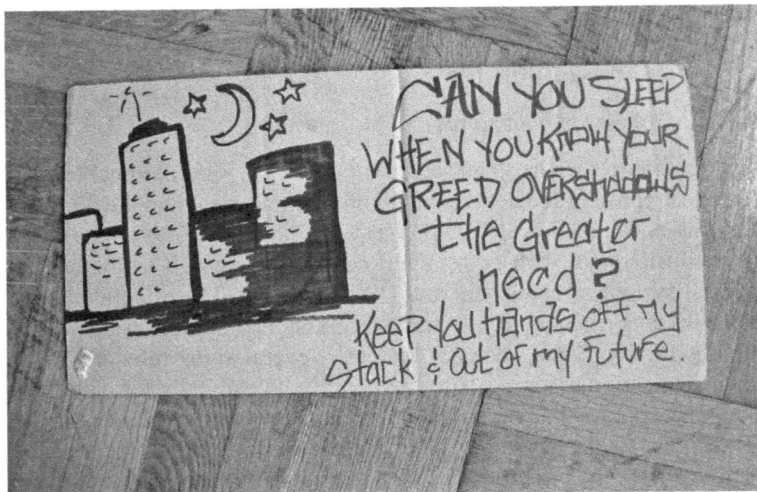

Figure 2.5 Protest sign from Occupy Wall Street with image. Unknown creator. Image from Amy Roberts' private collection (acquired by Tamiment Library in 2017).

Photograph by Kylie Message.

American domestic political and economic concerns where they call for specific actions. The references to an international context are typically more general in regard to the demand being sought, and almost exclusively directed to 'Egypt' ('SUPPORT EGYPT'S DEMOCRACY!'; 'STAND WITH EGYPT!'; 'EGYPT IS OUR ALLY!'; 'END MILITARY TRIALS IN EGYPT!'). There is a very small minority of generic 'global' messages; these focus on environmental concerns.

Discussion

Main themes:

1.   Visual style as Occupy Wall Street trademark
2.   Authenticity of messaging

1. Visual style: Attention!

A visual call to attention made midway through 2011 promoted the start date of Occupy Wall Street on September 17 (Beeston 2011; Beirut 2012).

The call came in the form of a poster produced by Adbusters that had high-quality production graphics and a single question 'What is Our One Demand?' One commentator responded to the poster by saying:

> The presence of AdBuster's beautiful graphics is very confusing because they feel like someone has to be behind this. Occupy presents a question. If anarchism is a real horizontal organization with people communicating and cooperating in new ways, why we are still getting images like this?
>
> (Benedetto 2011)

One answer to this question might be that the Adbusters image – sentimental, compelling, attractive – was produced before the occupation of Zuccotti Park occurred. It was designed as an incentive to capture the hearts and minds of potential occupiers, who it invoked to action – to turn up, 'with tent'. Another answer might be that the materiality of the call was less paradoxical than it was recognition that there would be material and logistic requirements if a resilient form of encampment was to take hold. The poster's invocation to 'bring tent' conveyed urgency as a practical, logistical, and material counterpoint to the mythical aspiration of the ballerina's carefully balanced pirouette:

What is Our One Demand?'
#OCCUPYWALLSTREET
SEPTEMBER 17th.
BRING TENT.

This poster is an exception that sits in contrast to the grassroots production and visual style of signs made by protesters during the occupation that followed. The visual arsenal that emerged throughout Occupy Wall Street differs from that of other activist movements, most of which are strongly associated with specific tropes.[6] For Occupy, text-based slogans such as 'We are the 99%' and numerous hashtag variations of #occupy proliferated rapidly as identifiers of the movement, probably more as a result of the social media reproduction they encouraged than any inherent symbolic visual features. Recurring images such as the raised closed fist and anarchist symbol do exist, but are at a minimum and speak more to the movement's shared history with other anti-establishment political protests than unique demands or specific historical precursors. No typeface guidelines, color standards, or official logos were prescribed, although text is predominantly capitalized, in *sans serif* font, and represented by single-color black or red permanent marker.

A further contradiction existed between the provocative imperative for a single demand by the corporate-style Adbusters poster and the multiple (sometimes competing) demands of the 99%.[7] In contrast to the poster's suggestion that there may be a ringleader behind the movement, the emphasis on collective, community-oriented action and political power that is evident in the collection's signs also raises questions about the frequent use of an active first-person 'I' on many of the signs. The contradiction between identifying the movement with a particular personhood – such as the iconic Guy Fawkes mask popularized by 'faceless hacking collective', Anonymous, which became a paradoxical face/no-face simulacra for the emerging movement (Ough 2015) – and an anonymous leaderless grassroots action representing the interests of the faceless masses was confusing to many middle American onlookers. This confusion was exacerbated in the context of the use of 'I'. 'Who is the "I" that made the sign?' asks another commentator:

> Who knows? Images that circulate on the Internet quickly lose any anchorage to their original context. All that seems certain is that this 'I' is one of the 'we,' one of those who understand themselves to be part of the multitude, the 99 percent.
>
> (Ough 2015)

The namelessness of the producers of these signs is also relevant in the context of the faceless masses of demonstrators that appear in photographs on social media and on syndicated news reports. While there is no provenance information available for the signs, they have at least two functional contexts: the specific camp at which they were produced and the demonstration at which they were raised, and the archive, where they take on a new life. The second archival life extends the image of protest that has been detached from any clear link to the identity of its maker such that the signs, more so than before, come to stand in for the (collective) 99% rather than any individual person or demand.

2. Enduring authenticity

Rather than offering an analogy to, or extension of, the Adbusters campaign, the signs produced during Occupy emphasize the experience-based realities and aspirations of occupiers.[8] In contrast to the traditional tropes of beauty and strength that are represented by the cinematic Adbusters poster, the protest signs stage heterogeneous identities and the unity of people who identify with the 99%. The image of collectivity presented by the signs was more performative and aspirational than it was a true reflection of life at Liberty Plaza. At some level, it may have simply reflected the desire to represent solidarity in the face of the systemic breakdowns and oppressions that led people to Occupy Wall Street. However, it did accurately reflect the collective social practices through which the signs were often produced. The signs marked proof that 'I am here', with others, occupying Wall Street, making signs with whatever materials are to hand.

The visual style and materiality of the signs indicate an organic sentiment that emerged during the occupation and privileged repurposed cardboard signs made *in situ* as having more value and authenticity than printed or professional-looking signs. Many of the signs show a very conspicuous attempt to demonstrate 're-use', with paper stuck over the top of previously used foam or cardboard signs. Signs made off site seemed to imply a distance from the occupation and access to funding or resources that could have perhaps been better utilized within the camp. One journalist described the visual style of messaging used on signs as a conscious action, saying:

> The protesters of Occupy Wall Street have been getting their act together for weeks now, improving food distribution and neighbor relations and media messaging. But their signs are as scruffy as the day they arrived. Pay the occupation a visit, and you're lucky to find a sheet of yellow construction paper hand-lettered in red magic marker. More common is a scrap of used cardboard box, unfolded and scribbled on in Sharpie. The message may be a bold 'Eat the Rich', but its delivery is a mess. And that, it seems, is often deliberate. 'I think what we're trying to emphasize is that normal people making their own signs can get the message across better than a bunch of perfectly-made signs'.
>
> (Gopnik 2011)

The suggestion that the handmade style is performative authentic is given further credence when we look more closely at individual signs as well as across the collection. I note, for example, that there were no spelling or grammar mistakes in the signs included in this group – none at all. While this likely represents the high proportion of educated middle-class participants in the movement (as represented, for example, by the sign that says 'It's hard out here for an educated whiteboy. Need to pay for grad school application. Anything helps') as well as the explicit attention to 'dress well, spell correctly, be aware that you're constantly on show' (Roberts n.d.i), it also evidences collective action in the sense that a process of proofreading is evident. It is clear where corrections have been made, and where letters or apostrophes have been later added (this, in addition to the practice of drafting the text in pencil first, is quite common). So although the signs appear to have been written rapidly, there is definite evidence of proofreading having been undertaken, which is consistent with the fact that at least in the early days the occupation had a station where sign-making was organized and supervised (Gopnik 2011).

The production of signs took place alongside other communication-oriented functions in the camp, including the high tech 'Tech Ops' (technical operations) Working Group, and operations by a press office and dedicated media center. They complemented ephemeral social media accounts by offering 'touchstones of what is true and knowable' (Edmundson 2015: n.p.; Tisdale 2011: 20). Members of the Occupy Archives Working Group recognized the archive's role as a holder of objects that would provide credible anchors to their original context.[9] Consistent with the research by Tisdale (2011) and reiterated by Ough (2015) and others,[10] they argued that the preservation of material culture would provide a more enduring record of the movement than digital records.[11]

The Occupy Archive includes a small collection of born-digital materials and the working group facilitated the collection of audio and visual oral histories (discussed in Roberts n.d.h: 7). They argued, however, that emphasis by the movement and the broader public on public outreach and social media was occurring at the expense of attention to self-representation and to a self-authored and controlled legacy for Occupy. Minutes from a meeting of the Archives Working Group held sometime between September 10 and November 7 record the group's view that rather than soliciting media attention, their purpose was to document what was happening (Roberts n.d.l).[12] In relation to a discussion about how to *materially* represent the diversity of opinions being expressed throughout the Occupation, the minutes state: 'Demands: No limit on ideas. Some people don't want demands but important to have some demands voiced but still acknowledge others' (*emphasis in original*). They encouraged Occupy participants to 'write them [the demands] down on pieces of paper all over plaza' to create a physical reminder of the movement's diversity of views and participation. A great many of these 'pieces of paper' are now included in the broader Occupy Archive, along with letters of support, artworks, buttons, patches, clippings, fliers, stickers, postcards, photographs, pamphlets, and gift vouchers for food and services (Tamiment Library and Robert F. Wagner Labor Archive 2018). The handwritten demands provide a further layer of material context to the physical signs that attracted widespread media interest.

Members of the Archives Working Group also agreed unanimously on the value of providing an evidence-based record of Occupy that would be used by traditional users of archives – academic researchers – as well as activists involved in future social movements who might want operational and process-based information. Their audience extended to include social researchers, including lawyers looking to assess primary sources for the purposes of prosecuting different claims. According to one working group member: 'The mainstream vision of an archivist is not that of somebody who protects [the] evidence' required by lawyers, but it was a reality for this working group, who would have no control over how that evidence was later used (see Roberts n.d.h.: 8).[13] About the veritable industry of publications generated by and about Occupy since 2011, another member commented:

> It would be great if all of the people who are writing these books can cite actual material instead of my cousin Judd whose friend was down there one day, who said that he said that his friend saw a sign that said 'Cops are Beautiful'!
>
> (interview at Roberts n.d.h: 26)

Conclusion: 'I'm so angry I made a sign'[14]

The signs were, by any measure, an effective mode of external public relations for the movement. This was not a coincidence, as image circulation was recognized as an important part of outreach.[15] They were a key attraction: 'On the pavement by the park, tourist photographers stood three deep', observed Taussig (2013: 25), before describing the performative still of the sign holder who 'is posing for photographers ... the sign is being made to pose for the camera' (Taussig 2013: 26). 'There are more cameras here than signs', reported Schneider (2013b: 25). Beyond the spectacle, the signs provided a talking point for people within the camp, as well as a hands-on activity that consolidated an embodied form of solidarity for many.[16] The signs captured the feeling of many in the movement that 'The problem is everywhere and looks different from every point of view' (van Gelder 2011a: 4). They represented the movement's strength at reaching out to people, many of whom felt compelled to carry signs for the first time, 'including some conservatives, along with union members who have been fighting a losing battle to maintain their standard of living' (van Gelder 2011a: 4).

Despite the rejection of a singular demand and a singular style of expression, the collection shows that the protesters were consistent in articulating a shared belief that the middle-class way of life was moving out of reach. The signs (complemented by the letters, images and oral histories in other parts of the Occupy Archive) tell stories of 'people who play by the rules, work long hours, study hard, and then find only low-wage jobs, often without health care coverage or prospects for a secure future' (van Gelder 2011a: 4). They show that behind the statistics and the analysis are real people who turned up, made signs, and became part of the movement.[17]

The signs also perform an idea of 'the personal is political' that may, like the raised closed fist, function as a recurrent symbol to indicate an association between Occupy and historical movements for civil rights (including those Mayo advocated for and sought to represent, as discussed in Chapter 1). And yet, whilst the ideal of collective action and political power was present in the production of the signs and performed at the protests in which they were held high, there remained a disjoint in the internal politics of the movement. This means that rather than representing an internal critique, signs like 'It's hard out here for an educated whiteboy' can be understood as signaling the political biases and personal inequities that were replicated within the lived experience of Occupy (Ashraf 2011). These internal fissures within the 'organization' of Occupy and within and between its working groups are the subject of the next chapter, and it is to those – and analysis of a different part of the archive (of internal documents and communications) – that I now turn.

Notes

1 Note Mitchell's use of the word 'impossible' (Mitchell 2012: 14).
2 My analysis of a small component of the collections modeled in this chapter illustrates the larger collections analysis exercise that was undertaken in order to write this book.
3 The material culture of social reform movements continues to accrue value; possibly as a result of being acquired by museums and archives nationally (Associated Press 2011; Judkis 2011; Schneider 2011; Helmore 2015). For historical context, see Message (2014).
4 The collections made by Occupy Wall Street Archives Working Group members are now primarily although not exclusively held by Tamiment Library.
5 As 'the radical potential of material culture is the endless possibility of rereading' (Hooper-Greenhill 1992: 215), there can be no singularly 'correct' way of classifying materials. I have employed just one of many approaches.
6 Materiality and iconography were signaled from the outset as significant components of the Occupy Wall Street movement, as indicated by the Adbusters posters that invited people to: '#OCCUPYWALLSTREET. SEPTEMBER 17th. BRING TENT'. The invocation to bring shelter indicated the intention for encampment and the practical role that material support would play during the occupation. Media was also a key part of the movement, but its analysis is beyond the scope of this small book.
7 Focused on symbolic action and persuasion, Vancouver-based magazine, *Adbusters* was criticized for appropriating the glossy style and form of the media and commercial products it attacks (particularly because it did not participate in Occupy Wall Street grassroots actions beyond generating initial interest in the movement). Its focus on creating symbolic imaginaries that are affective forms of persuasion and relationship building was articulated by Senior Editor, Micah White:

> 'We rely on passionate words, pertinent facts and beautiful art to try to provoke epiphanies! That's what it's all about!' 'We didn't tell people to go out to Wall Street,' explained White. 'All we said was, "Wouldn't it be beautiful if people went to Wall Street," and then they felt inspired and made it their own. It's not something that Adbusters did; it's something we did together'.
> (Quoted in Beeston 2011)

8 The movement's acknowledgment of the impact of material culture is also evident in the production and distribution throughout the months of October and

November 2011 of tens of thousands of physical A3 size print copies of the *Occupied Wall Street Journal* to provide news about the encampment to participants and others. Many copies of these were collected for physical repositories (including at the Museum of the City of New York and Interference Archive, for example, as well as the Tamiment collection). Nathan Schneider argues that distribution of the print papers offered a form of human interaction that complemented the movement's focus on high tech communications. 'Physical print, like the physical occupation itself', was, he later recalled, 'like pinching yourself in a dream, [it] was also a special kind of assurance that this was really happening' (Schneider 2013b: 83).

9 The Archives Working Group frequently said that their collection would benefit future activists who could access and refer to materials as resources, and that it would preserve Occupy's legacy in the terms of its participants. An additional benefit exists for collecting institutions, including museums as well as archives, which 'need to develop object-centered historical experiences for visitors that are not only educational but also unique, memorable, moving, provocative. We talk about this a lot but we aren't doing it enough' (Tisdale 2011: 20). I thank Anna Edmundson for making this important point, which relates to discussions about contemporary cause-based collecting explored in other parts of this book.

10 The value attributed to the production of signs in the camp reflects ongoing research that has indicated that 'the increase in digital versions of objects actually enhances the value of in-person encounters with tangible, real things' (Tisdale 2011: 20). In 2008, a survey of 5000 visitors to living history sites in the USA found that those surveyed expressed a strong desire to commune with historically authentic objects (Wilkening and Donnis 2008), while a subsequent survey aimed specifically at young audiences (in their early twenties) reported that: 'seeing stuff online only made them want to see the real objects in person even more' (Wilkening 2009: n.p.).

11 One working group member (see Roberts n.d.h: 7) advocated for hard copies of everything.

12 These minutes are included in a small notebook written during the occupation, dated from September 17 to November 7 2011 (Roberts n.d.l). Notes from one meeting during the occupation recorded the view that the archive is important 'if someone in future wants primary source info on this mvmt not the media perspective' (Roberts n.d.l).

13 However, as Howard Besser of the Activist Archivists group also points out, evidence can be used both for and against occupiers in court-based proceedings:

> Mr. Besser said he has felt the need to warn protesters that the photos and videos they share could be used by authorities policing the protests, as well as scholars. 'These videos have been used by police and by lawyers in cases', said Mr. Besser, in an interview. He feels that archivists have an ethical responsibility to warn participants, even if that means some will hold back their photos and videos. 'It's not in our best interest', he notes.
>
> (Young 2012)

14 Phrase taken from a sign quoted in Taussig (2013: 38).

15 View reported by the Diversity/Outreach/Media Breakaway group of the Arts and Labor Working Group (Arts and Labor Meeting Minutes 11/22/11,

http://www.nycga.net/group-documents/arts-labor-meeting-minutes-112211/, link no longer live).

16 In a speech delivered at Liberty Plaza on October 6, 2011, Naomi Klein said: 'My favorite sign here says, "I care about you." In a culture that trains people to avoid each other's gaze, to say "Let them die," that sign carries a deeply radical statement' (speech reproduced in the *Occupied Wall Street Times*; see Klein 2011).

17 These stories are extensively represented in paper-based collections at Tamiment Library (Tamiment Library and Robert F. Wagner Labor Archive 2018).

3   Organizing action
Archiving Occupy

The Occupy Archives Working Group's mission was consistent with the movement's aim to control its image and the way its image would be used into the future. The group's outlook exemplified the shift that was described by journalist Sarah van Gelder during the occupation: 'The Occupy Wall Street Movement is not just demanding change. It is also transforming how we, the 99%, see ourselves' (van Gelder 2011a: 11–12). And yet, while no one could credibly argue that the material culture expressions of protest – the pizza-box signs, messages on placards, T-shirt slogans, artworks, and ephemera created by protestors – were not intended to exist as a kind of activist public relations, the collection of these materials by the Occupy Wall Street Archives Working Group was not widely supported within the movement. This means that the group's activities have not been considered in relation to Occupy's interest in authoring its own history. This chapter addresses this oversight by arguing that the self-documentation component of the Occupy Archive offers a collectively produced autoethnography of the intersecting structures and practices employed by activist communities and archivists.

The group's experience of collection development also demonstrated the need for internal activism as a way of convincing the broader Occupy Wall Street movement of the benefits of activist archiving. Persuasion required a strategic form of activist public relations that targeted two audiences: an external public that would engage with a resultant collection of materials representing Occupy, and internal communities of activist peers within Occupy. Discussion of the strategies used to communicate with each of these target cohorts reveals a disjoint between Occupy Wall Street's concerns with image control on the one hand, and its suspicion, on the other hand, of the process of self-archiving that was being undertaken by the Occupy Wall Street Archives Working Group.

This chapter examines why the working group privileged the collection of self-documentation records and archives in the context of creating an

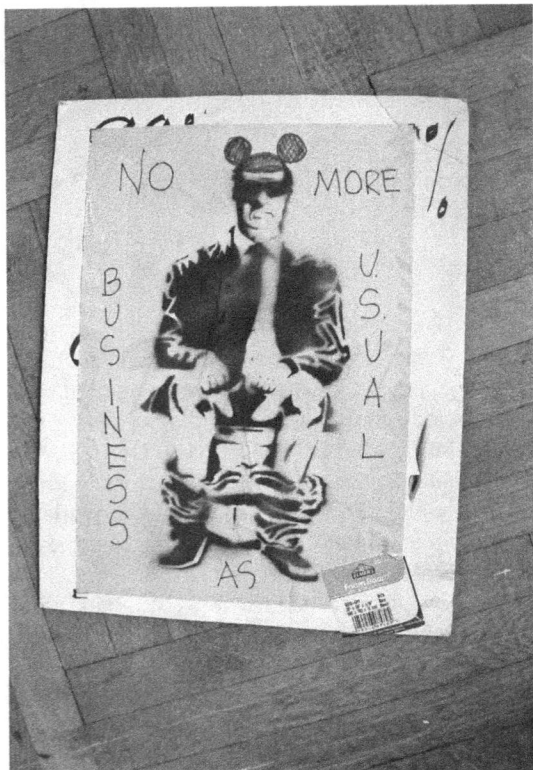

Figure 3.1 'NO MORE BUSINESS AS USUAL' re-used protest sign from Occupy
Wall Street. Unknown creator. Image from Amy Roberts' private
collection (acquired by Tamiment Library in 2017).

Photograph by Kylie Message.

enduring historical narrative for, of, and about Occupy Wall Street. I show
that while the aim of the Archives Working Group was to maintain control of the movement's image, reputation, and legacy, they also, even more
importantly, promoted the collection as an activist resource that reflected the
first-hand experience of history in the making. Rather than just existing as a
commemoration of a past event, the collection was intended to function as a
'living resource' (a 'means' rather than an 'end') that could continue to shape
and influence the views of constituents both within and outside the movement. The working group sought to challenge institutional power by modeling an alternative approach to activist archiving that privileged collaboration

and relationship building, and in so doing, sought to challenge dominant misconceptions within Occupy about what archiving meant. Rather than having any pretensions for neutrality, the Archives Working Group believed in the archive's potential to represent the process of relationship building that occurs in their production of what I have referred to, following Star (1999), as an autoethnography of an anti-institutional infrastructure. They also documented the anti-institutional processes and practices that emerged throughout Occupy Wall Street, to offer a representation of internal social movement structures that complement the more familiar public face of the movement discussed in previous chapters. Their record of process combines with the popular material culture products of Occupy reproduced through media imagery to generate a fuller historical record of Occupy Wall Street.

Public relations advocacy

This chapter has been informed by activist public relations, which is a form of communication studies scholarship that has some affinity with cultural studies approaches to understanding interactions between individual and collective actors and events. Activist public relations focuses on a process of stakeholder management that T. W. Coombs and S. J. Holladay (2010: 4) call 'the management of mutually influential relationships within a web of constituency relationships'. While members of the Archives Working Group did not explicitly articulate their role in public relations terms, they were certainly motivated by the intention to maintain control over the way the movement was preserved and subsequently used in collections held by archives, libraries, museums, and other repositories. For example, in contrast to the expectation that processes of documentation generate a neutral and objective recording of the 'truth' of any event for historical purposes, the working group sought to contribute a direct form of embodied participant action and reflection to the movement. They wanted to establish archives that would serve as well as document the movement (Bold 2012b). Their belief that activist archiving could be a manifestation and extension of the social reform movement guided their pragmatic approach to building a collection that would exist as both a record of, and legacy for, the movement, on the movement's own terms.

Their attention to creating an image for general (non-Occupy-aligned) public consumption was supplemented by the task of making a case to Occupy for internal support of the archive. Their approach to activism was consistent with Kevin Moloney's (2005) argument that a fundamental premise of advocacy is the endeavor to alter the behaviors of others, where 'others' are usually defined as a mainstream 'general public' and its government offices and representatives (including city, state, and national museums and collecting institutions). However, the target of the working group's public relations strategy extended to an internal 'other' group of peers that included the New York City General Assembly, which was the primary decision-making forum at Occupy Wall Street. Persuading the General Assembly required 'sustained strategic attempts to influence relationships' (Coombs and Holladay 2012: 348) that typically took the approach of educating members about the role that archives can play as an activist-oriented public relation strategy. Understanding the process of communication and strategic relationship building within the internal constituency networks of Occupy Wall Street is essential to a discussion about activist public relations because the long-term preservation of the collection was contingent upon funding and approval by the General Assembly. Without this it could not exist, and the legacy of the movement would be left for others to represent and control.[1]

Collections and archives are widely recognized as representational forms of authority that have historically been associated with propaganda and selective, often governmental, frameworks and agendas (Bennett 1995; Message 2018b). However, they have not been considered in the context of public relations strategies, or according to the field of literature that now exists to analyze this form of communication (Coombs and Holladay 2010; L'Etang 2016). This is an oversight because contemporary collections-based research is characterized by an increasing emphasis on relationship building and stakeholder management that is also at the heart of critical literature around activist public relations (Flinn and Alexander 2015). Although I do not delve deeply into the disciplinary context of activist public relations and communication studies, this chapter brings the stakeholder and constituent focus of this scholarship into dialogue with community and agenda-based collections to examine some ways in which the collections and archives created by the Occupy Wall Street Archives Working Group worked both for and perhaps, in the opinion of some in the movement, against, Occupy Wall Street.

The first section of the chapter explores how the material collected by the Archives Working Group contributed to Occupy's goal of maintaining authority over its external image. I show that the collections provided a positive form of public relations that communicated directly with a general audience who would otherwise become familiar with representations of Occupy authored by the staff of public museums, libraries, and archives that were also acquiring materials from the site. The second part of the chapter examines the more complex internal public relations strategies that occurred between the Archives Working Group and the General Assembly. It considers why public relations strategies were necessary to facilitate what was essentially a form of internal advocacy. The chapter's final section looks at the long-term plight of the archives in relation to debates about independence versus institutionalization.

In recognition of Cook's argument that archives exist 'as curatorial process, as institution, as profession, as assumptions and beliefs, and as archival records' (Cook 2011: 615), previous chapters of this book have honed in on the object-based products – the 'content' – of the archive. They profiled collections of material culture, 'ephemera', and items that one would more typically expect to find in a museum collection than in an archive or library. The focus of this chapter is on records that conform more readily to traditional definitions of materials held by archives as repositories for communication-based texts. These include records associated with self-documentation and bureaucracy such as meeting schedules, agendas, protocols, budget requests, drafts proposals, revisions, remittances, quotes for storage and supplies, contact details, requests for attendance at meetings, and so on. These paper-based, primarily handwritten records may, on the face of it, be considered less exciting than the orange police net introduced in Chapter 1, or the unprocessed signs described in Chapter 2.[2] They do, however, evidence crucial processes employed by the working group in pursuit of their goal of creating a different kind of activist archive that would account authentically for activist events by engaging effectively and independently with conventional forms of archiving infrastructure that formed the broader context in which they sought to have relevance.

My sources for this chapter are the Occupy Wall Street Archives Working Group Records (Tamiment Library and Robert F. Wagner Labor Archive 2018), which hold the Occupy Wall Street Archives Working Group's organizational documents, and the working group's online Google group discussion forum maintained through most of 2012 and 2013.[3] Although the question of whether the group of collections that I have designated as the Occupy Archive is or was proto- or anti-institutional (and whether this necessarily infers a dichotomous relationship to 'independence') will be explored throughout the chapter, it is critical to note at the outset the working group's mission to collect materials *by, about, and for* Occupy.[4] The group's approach to collecting materials for both external and internal stakeholders reflected their two main audiences. It also demonstrates the difficulty of categorizing collection activities according to the dichotomy that is, as Terry Cook and Joan M. Schwartz argue, frequently applied to archives:

> There is a basic dichotomy of archives being, on the one hand, heritage places with documentary records that embody historical memory and humanist culture, and archives being, on the other hand, bureaucratic by-products that encompass administrative evidence and public accountabilities. ... Yet neither tradition sees archives as sites of contested meaning and of social interpretation, although the dichotomy itself is proof of the contested nature of control of the past.
>
> (Cook and Schwartz 2002: 181)

The archives at the heart of this book exemplify the connectedness of the terms of affect and experience on the one hand, *and* evidence and accountability on the other hand, in a case study that is exemplary for simultaneously representing and contributing to a moment of contemporary contestation. The Occupy Archive represents the experience and affect of participation in the movement, the production of documentation that sought to disrupt the 'business as usual' model of mainstream archives, and the corporate culture and political instruments these archives were criticized as serving.

The actions of the Occupy Wall Street Archives Working Group – both in collecting protest signs[5] and in documenting the processes involved in forming the movement – play a key role in demonstrating how the knowledge practices of social movements contribute different ways of addressing the failure of 'business as usual' conventions (Chesters 2012: 146). For example, the working group attempted to reveal the 'mediated nature of archives as appraised and selected records, as curatorial institutions' (Cook 2011: 611). Its aim in doing this was to show the sticky and formative processes by which archives result from and contribute to broader forms of social activity and experience, including institutions of governance that organize ideas and records into standardized forms. The process of rupturing the business as usual model could only, perhaps ironically given the Occupy movement's predilection for revolution, be undertaken from 'the inside out', by re-purposing the tools of the (archiving) trade to reach new (activist) outcomes and audiences. It was inevitable that this process needed to acknowledge the agency of archivists to critique the archival products that result from their efforts and decisions.[6] It was perhaps also inevitable that this led to image problems for the Archives Working Group, which was viewed with suspicion by some members of the General Assembly and other working groups.

Authority over image: 'External' activism

The Archives Working Group created collections that would preserve the authority of Occupy Wall Street over its image and legacy. Much of the material culture that was collected was the typical residue of protest created as a form of activist public relations to persuade non-Occupy audiences of the legitimacy of their claims. In addition to oral histories and audio-visual records, it included material that was widely represented in news media reporting, swept up by Sanitation services for disposal, or confiscated by police. This material typically generated responses like: 'the posters, God, they were so good!' (Harcourt 2013: 66) Roberts argued that a broad and multi-focused approach to collecting was appropriate for reflecting the changing mood of people within the movement. This approach to collecting

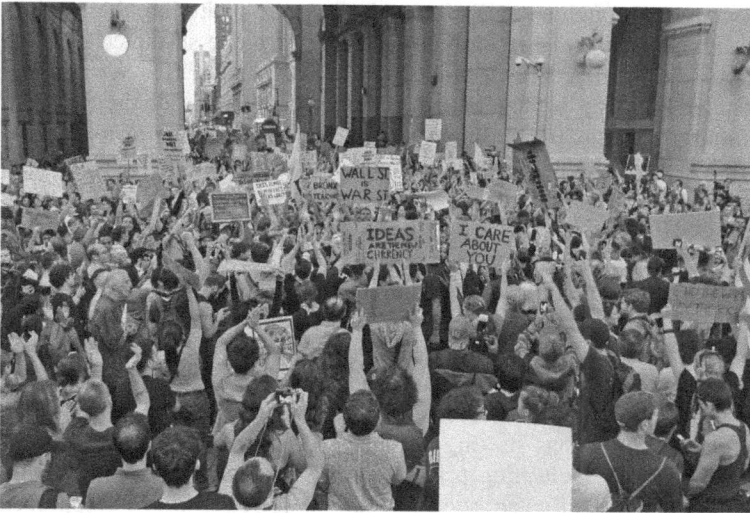

Figure 3.2 'Day 14 Occupy Wall Street, September 30, 2011'.

Photograph by David Shankbone. Image used according to a Creative Commons license, https://commons.wikimedia.org/wiki/Occupy_Wall_Street#/media/File:Day_14_Occupy_ Wall_Street_September_30_2011_Shankbone_47.JPG

led members of the Archives Working Group (and the broader Occupy movement) to debate the value of preserving material that was ephemeral, often damaged, usually impossible to ascribe authorship for, and difficult at that time to assess as being either representative or unique. Their debates reiterated the conversations about value attribution that was also occurring in other archiving communities at this time. As explored in previous chapters, the group's approach to collecting emerged primarily as a result of circumstance and opportunity, a point made also by Roberts:

> As you know there was a raid on the occupation that started at 1:00am on Tuesday morning. Fortunately, our archival material was stored offsite. There were many things that we wanted to collect that were destroyed however. That is of course because almost everything was destroyed including the library. I think this highlights the importance of the oral history project. People have been allowed back in the park but not to set up tents or tarps. People are still making signs and I think it is important that we collect these as they reflect people's moods and thoughts about the latest developments.
>
> (Roberts 2011b)

There were further concerns that without financial support provided directly by Occupy or through an affiliation with a partner institution, the archives could not be established in the first instance, let alone sustained over the long term. Some members argued in favor of a digital archive over a material one as one way of counteracting the precariousness of the repository's future (Roberts 2011c; Sulehka 2011; Ng 2011). Many of the typical materials collected, including protest signs, banners, and other ephemera, are also commonly found in 'protest and reform' collections in established museums. However, of this practice, Sellie *et al.* (2015: 456) said: 'Any archive can collect objects made by activists. But this process does not automatically signify that this collection establishes a relationship between the archive and the community that it draws materials from'.

A closer look at the Archives Working Group's mission statement and collections demonstrates an explicit rejection of attempts to 'glamorize activism' which, along with nostalgia, is a characteristic often present in larger public collections seeking to make Occupy materials bend to conform with specific collecting priority areas.[7] In contrast with the highly curated collections of established institutions (refer to Mayo's approach described in Chapter 1), the working group's grassroots strategy for collecting reinforced the importance of inclusion and sought, where possible, to attribute authority to creators and those involved in the movement. Their tactics, more readily affiliated with activist archiving, proactively worked to demonstrate the falsity of assumptions that activism 'is necessarily a homogeneous category' (L'Etang 2016: 207). The group's multifarious approach to collection development also reflected a shift away from perceptions that the student protest movements and social critiques of the 1960s and 1970s contributed to the formation of fixed identities where conservative, corporate-sponsored public relations was defined against radical societal critiques (Coombs and Holladay 2012). Not only does this historical dichotomy erroneously pigeonhole activist public relations as something defined categorically as that which corporate and government public relations is not, but it also represents activist public relations as a homogenous and singular set of approaches dedicated to progressing an uncontested mission, which it is not.

Emphasizing the pluralism and heterogeneity of archives and archiving as a way to reject the assumptions and dichotomy that have typically defined activism (and what it is not) is a strategy that invites consideration of who the Archives Working Group's target audience actually was. This approach allows recognition that the public-facing collections, which offer a self-representational image of Occupy (as a mainstream-oriented public relations strategy for the movement) are, in fact, less significant than the collections (primarily of documentation, correspondences, records of decision-making and the like) that sought to function as a form of public relations generated by activists *for* activists. Rather than exclusively including the disposable products of the movement (signs, banners, and so on and so forth), these collections typically include material that documents the experience of living at or contributing to the Occupy movement from the perspective of 'insiders'.

There are two reasons the collection process may have fallen into adopting a public relations strategy to target an ('insider') activist stakeholder cohort. The first was functional. It sought to provide an open educational resource that could be actively used by other protest movements – such that, for example, placards could be subsequently borrowed, re-used, and returned to the archive (Evans, Perricci, and Roberts 2014).[8] The second reason was ideological, and related to the working group's commitment to producing a record of internal interactions and debate within Occupy Wall Street that would contribute to continuing accountability within the movement. The collections were, in short, designed as communication strategies that would advocate for and maintain authority over the image of Occupy. Although they targeted different constituents – an external 'public' on the one hand, and other activist groups, on the other hand – this comparison shows that they shared the concern with maintaining control over the movement's messages in the short term (representation in current exhibitions and media) and long term (re-use by other activists).

Prefigurative politics: 'Lost my job, found an occupation'[9]

Articulated by popular slogans such as 'This is not a protest, this is a process', and 'This is what democracy looks like', the global Occupy movement has been described as 'prefigurative' (Graeber 2011 and 2013). It aimed to explore and enact new forms of social organization and governance in such a way that allowed activists to 'model or *prefigure* the future society [including archival institutions and practice] at micro-level that they hope to realize at a societal level, thereby instantiating radical institutional transformation in and through practice' (Reinecke 2018: 1300; Harcourt 2013: 73). The prefigurative politics embodied by the Archives Working Group was grounded in an everyday politics of practice that sought to enact a desired future society and archival practice in the 'here and now' that would disrupt the reproduction of institutionalized structures that sustain and reproduce inequalities.

Starting from the premise that the means *is* the end goal, Occupy experimented with establishing new political structures based on horizontality, self-organization, and inclusivity. These same principles guided the Archives Working Group's use and adaptation of organizational and professional archival strategies to 'mobilize resources, promote change-oriented collective action [and structures], and challenge institutional authority' (Reinecke 2018: 1300). The working group's attention to the everyday infrastructures of collective action (attending to both the small-scale quotidian needs of the camp as well as participating in the movement's consensus-based decision-making processes) was motivated by a belief that institutional change was only possible if the reproduction of power and injustice by everyday mechanisms was reconfigured – in practice – according to a new set of goals.

The Archives Working Group retained links to the infrastructure and tools of the professional archiving sector, which they adapted to suit the alternative prefigurative political environment of Liberty Plaza. Their engagement with multiple organizational structures is also consistent with the process-oriented approach of 'expressive' (prefigurative) politics, which recognizes that 'change at the level of practice requires actors to remain inside the practice and change institutions from the inside out' (Reinecke 2018: 1302). Their 'inside' was a place of exceptionality where participants, exempt from prevailing norms and prescribed institutionalized perceptions, created 'a vantage point for the critique of the status quo (Feigenbaum *et al.* 2013: 191 quoted in Reinecke 2018: 1313) that could lead to new individual and collective political subjectivities through the rejection or reconfiguration of norms, methods, and conventions. Working to effect change from 'inside' the movement, members of the working group (many of whom were professionally trained archivists) explored a form of activist archiving that demanded legitimacy from both activist and archival sectors.

Bureaucratic byproducts

At its most rudimentary, infrastructure refers to basic physical and organizational structures, facilities and conventions necessary for the operation of a society or enterprise. These can include large-scale physical forms, such as buildings, roads, and power supplies but, as archival collections demonstrate, collections of documentary outputs also exist as outcomes or artifacts that reflect *and* constitute the procedures, mechanisms, and conventions – the infrastructure – of organizational work. While museum and archive studies scholars are familiar with discussions about institutions (in relation to 'national', 'public', 'collecting' institutions, etc.), the term 'organization', although less frequently used, is almost never defined. I take my understanding of these terms from Gary Bouma, who explains:

> Institutions are sets of norms which apply across a variety of specific organisations. Organisations are structures of social relationship social actors arranged in positions and roles; usually, but not always,

deliberately arranged and designed to achieve some end. Institutions provide normative [that is, regulatory] environments [rules] shaping the activities of organisations.

(Bouma 1998: 232)

Internal collections of documentation, registration forms, correspondences, donor agreements, skills-based workshops on oral history, guidelines for collections preservation, recommendations on what to do if arrested, records of decision-making, and so on and so forth – the 'bureaucratic byproducts' (Cook and Schwartz 2002: 181) of archives and activism alike – are less 'glamorous' than the collections of signs, posters, and T-shirts, which more readily capture the imagination of external audiences. Yet these artifacts of 'behind-the-scenes' mechanisms of meaning production also function as a critical form of public relations generated by activists *for* activists because they contribute to the social organization *and* the institutional and proto-institutional documentation produced out of the attempt to maintain account-ability for and on behalf of the movement. These collections contribute to as well as record the infrastructure of archiving and activism, and evidence the points at which these (often antagonistic) systems come into contact.

The collection's documents and records can be read on face value for the textual information conveyed through their content. They represent 'official' positions in the form of mission statements, and provide a record of deci-sions made. They also function concurrently as constitutive materials that actively contribute to and record the often-invisible negotiations occurring between individual agency, the challenges of collective forms of consensus-making, and the traditional hierarchical institutional arrangements involved in the establishment of new archival practices and organizational standards or expectations. The working group's foregrounding and reclaiming (often though re-appropriation) of 'bureaucratic byproducts', including professional archiving standards around collections development, acquisition, process-ing and preservation, and ethical codes focused on determining agency and authority for materials, was consistent with Occupy's commitment to prefig-urative politics. The group's processes for exploring and modeling a horizon-tal approach to documentation, collection, and preservation was consistent with Occupy's insistence that the organizational processes and structures of the movement be transparent and accessible so as to enable further discussion and engagement. This was made evident at a public forum at which Roberts invited participants to donate materials: '[T]his will document our side of the story and history ... If anyone has any notes or drafts of proposal with hand-writing we are asking for you to donate it'. The archive would be important for people who 'in future want primary source info on this mvmt [movement] not the media perspective', she explained (Roberts n.d.l).

The Archives Working Group had an explicitly political purpose, understood by many of its members as a function of its unique ability to offer a social movement perspective to the documentation of the movement. Its remit reflected Occupy's aim to target cultural as well as economic, health, welfare, and other forms of governmental infrastructure for transformation by focusing on social practices around collaboration, community building, and network development. It also embodied the movement's aim to explore participatory democratic process as the basis for creating new formal organizational models. Occupiers more broadly understood that an attention to infrastructure, even the boring, invisible, or taken-for-granted elements of infrastructure, was necessary to progress their aim of exploring what might happen if the Occupy model of horizontalism were 'pushed into every venue of civil society, [with the goal of] eventually supplanting the roots of our representative democracy system' (Bauer 2012). They recognized that the task of transforming institutions, organizations, and networks from the bottom up stood 'in radical contrast to how we normally conduct business' (Barber 2012). The Archives Working Group, however, believed that in addition to telling us something about the collecting process used by activist archivists or curators, the movement's material bureaucratic byproducts (collections, in this case) would provide evidence of the intention, role, and potential of Occupy to influence all the meta-structures, social arrangements, hierarchies, networks and technologies with which it interacts and intersects, and over which it aims to have an influence. This view was a result of the group's embeddedness in a network of activity and tool- and resource-based infrastructures that sat across and included both the Occupy movement and the archiving sector.

Although the working group's primary mission was to represent the viewpoint and authority of Occupy participants, they also believed in the importance of creating records that could gain leverage within different, sometimes conflicting contexts and communities of practice and reception that have their own established norms, expectations, and frameworks for meaning production. Their dialogic model worked across their key contexts of the Occupy movement (the practice of prefigurative politics), the archiving profession and sector (to which they sought to model a radical reinvention of practice), and the broader general public. The intersectional nature of their work led to contestation where the rationale for the development of certain processes was not clear, recognized, or respected. However, their resulting collections of sometimes 'boring things' (Star 1999: 377) demonstrate that while 'infrastructure' exists in its own right and in relation to specific ideological drivers (such as the Occupy movement), it also functions concurrently as a component of a larger assemblage (for example, professional standards) that contributes to an almost limitless field of data beyond that (such as society).[10]

Working group members recognized that the infrastructure of archiving, and particularly of activist archiving, can be difficult to discern because it is 'sunk into and inside of other structures, social arrangements, and technologies' (Star 1999: 381; Graeber 2013: 290). In response to this challenge, the collection presented a material attempt to embody the experience and processes that contributed to the constitution of the prefigurative archive's social structure. It also sought to articulate the overarching decisions and principles that were created by, and later submerged within, the new infrastructure that resulted from this process. As such, the collection both reflects and documents the workings of proto-organizational life, including formal and informal relations; uncodified activities and formal communication mechanisms; 'institutional' power plays; and personal and interpersonal, racial, gender and class-based inequalities and dynamics. It also sought to simultaneously produce new standards for organizational order (meeting agendas and minutes as well as collection development 'policies' and the like) appropriate to the formal organizational tasks at hand.

A comparison of the infrastructural processes, resources, and conventions of anti-institutional and institutional forms of collecting shows that the goals of bottom-up participatory social movements such as Occupy and formal, state-regulated, legal-rational bureaucracies and institutions such as the Smithsonian Institution are not mutually exclusive. It also shows that the processes of each contribute to the implementation of shared infrastructural networks, instruments and conventions, even where the driving ideological principles are not the same. The working group's embeddedness within different communities of practice led to some degree of conflict with and alienation from both. The main point of contention from the perspective of Occupy was the group's acceptance and use of professional standards as a mechanism for establishing legitimacy for the collection as a reflection of the movement. However, even while the dual positioning of the Archives Working Group led to conflict between its aims and those of the broader movement on some occasions, it was a fundamental part of their 'occupation'. The group's complex insider/outsider status and attendant problems were not unique to the Occupy Archives Working Group. Of a different group, Reinecke explains that where activists focused 'on enacting these ideals only among themselves, they risk building isolated, inward-looking communities that escape rather than change wider society'. In relation to her example of 'Occupy the Farm', she explains that in preaching only to the converted, 'like-minded activists created an agricultural commons but isolated themselves from wider institutional challenges'. This can, she says 'make organizing expressive of desired change, but fails to leverage change outside' (Reinecke 2018: 1302).

In the final instance, the 'bureaucratic byproducts' created by the Archives Working Group were understood by those within the group as having a great deal more significance and centrality than the phrase 'byproducts' suggests. Working group members also understood the documentary infrastructure that constituted the archive as being a central mechanism for maintaining agency and authority over the ways the movement and its processes would be represented into the future. Whereas documentary infrastructure usually refers to conventions and standards that regulate practices according to institutional priorities, the Occupy Archive sought to create an archive that would enable new practices reflective of new political subjectivities emerging from a prefigurative experimentation and modeling of regulations, activities, processes, debates, behaviors, materials, and technologies.

Occupy infrastructure – 'This place is organized!'[11]

Occupiers beyond the Archives Working Group also expressed widespread commitment to the idea that the issues at the heart of infrastructure are 'intensely political' and related to social justice (Bauer 2012). These issues included how (and where) resources are cultivated and distributed (and by and with whom), and how technologies are located, built, and installed. This emphasis was borne out by the daily realities of life at Liberty Plaza, where the basic infrastructure of communal living was a pressing concern. Whilst the Archives might have attracted relatively modest media attention (probably because its collections were held off-site and because it's collecting infrastructure was considered non-essential), other 'service areas', like the park's sanitation area, kitchen, electricity generators, library, and media center, which were all highly visible, provided frequent topics of fascination for bystanders. Attention to the functional components of running the camp occurred largely for pragmatic reasons. Any occupation of a site by a group of people across a period of time will create practical challenges about how infrastructure (resources, regulations, norms) can be accessed, adapted, and distributed to suit the acute needs of sheltering people. These challenges extend to influence the longer-term affective project of community-building and consolidating a commitment to the cause, as required for any movement's longevity.

After it was all over, some commentators evaluated the movement as having succeeded in 'encouraging people to embrace the idea of a "society of care"' (Bauer 2012). Others argued that it modeled a reformed political process. Almost all assessments included analysis of the movement's instrumental impact or interventions within some aspect of social infrastructure. Miller, for example, recounts the perception by participants that Occupy provided 'a real, and striking, alternative to simply pulling levers to choose between candidates selected in advance by others, and often selected precisely in order to defend the interests of an oligarchic elite'. His observation continues:

> 'There is an energy and an amazing consensus process working with 50+ people in general assembly several times a day', wrote another participant a few days later, marveling at how the group was successfully making decisions about how to run the occupation – from when to do marches, to how to communicate, to ideas about food, art, entertainment, and all kinds of issues that anyone can bring up.
>
> (Miller 2018)

Examining the Archives Working Group's networks and relationships with the Occupy movement and traditional archival institutions as rationalized, collective structures also enables the creation of a productive dialogue between theoretical work from various fields of research, including social movement studies, organizational studies (Star 1999), and archival studies (Stoler 2002). A definition of social movement studies that is appropriate to the specific context of the global Occupy movement comes from Catherine Eschle (2018). She says that narrative accounts are another form of informal organizational infrastructure based on social relations. When these are shared between participants of social movements they become fundamental to what a movement *is*. Activist accounts of the endings of movements merit particular critical scrutiny, she says, because 'they constitute efforts to fix rival understandings of participant experience and of the possibilities for future activism' (Eschle 2018: 527). This approach is complemented by organizational studies, which is 'the examination of how individuals construct organizational structures, processes, and practices and how these, in turn, shape social relations and create institutions that ultimately influence people' (Clegg and Bailey 2008). Interdisciplinary dialogue between these fields can offer a productive contribution to attempts to break down the dichotomous relationships usually attributed to collective behavior where social movements are grouped with threatening forms of collective disorder and moral panic like crowds, riots, and gangs. Formal organizations such as national or state archival institutions are positioned as antagonistic to these collective forms on the grounds that they are instruments of legal-rational bureaucracy and government regulation designed to 'stamp out the particularism of individual and group dynamics and reinforce uniformity of behavior' (Weber and King 2014: 490).

Other useful ways to engage with the challenges of competing infrastructural forms in a prefigurative environment are provided by cultural theory approaches that seek to analyze the infrastructure created and consolidated by both social movements and formal institutional sites of governance. These approaches focus attention on systems analysis and often employ organizational autoethnography methods (*Culture and Organization* 2007).[12] Similarly, and despite working in different primary fields (information studies and archive studies respectively), Susan Leigh Star and Ann Laura Stoler share an emphasis on working across and with the conflicts arising from theoretical and practical sites of infrastructure. They both address problems that can only be answered through recourse to embedded forms of knowledge and experience, and advocate the use of ethnographic methods for systems analysis work. 'How', asks Star (1999: 379), 'do we understand the ecology of work as affected by standardization and classification?' Stoler (2002 and 2010) similarly invokes us to adapt our understanding of archives (as forms of standardization and classification) to be means or process driven and thereby more responsive to the context in which they operate. This is what is meant by Stoler's invocation to engage with archives as subjects rather than sources.[13]

Star and Stoler identify their subjects – systems infrastructure and archives respectively – as fundamentally embedded, relational concepts that influence and are in turn 'shaped by the conventions of a community of practice' (Star 1999: 382). These characteristics are also key features of the collections produced by the Occupy Wall Street Archives Working Group, which were shaped to reflect and communicate across the current conventions of multiple communities of practice that participants were working in. Star's observations about infrastructure are also applicable to discussions about collections:

> People commonly envision infrastructure as a system of substrates – railroad lines, pipes and plumbing, electrical power plants, and wires. It is by definition invisible, part of the background for other kinds of work. It is ready-to-hand. … [For example] … For a railroad engineer, the rails are not infrastructure but topic. For the person in a wheelchair, the stairs and doorjamb in front of a building are not seamless subtenders of use, but barriers. One person's infrastructure is another's topic, or difficulty.
>
> (Star 1999: 380)

Pluralistic self-documentation practices were employed by the Archives Working Group, but this statement has broader relevance to archives in general. Historians, for example, might identify archives as being akin to Star's 'system of substrates', where they function as an enabler, as 'part of the background for other kinds of work'. This contrasts with the perspective taken by the archivist, who engages with the archive as the primary topic (or subject) for consideration and analysis.[14] Furthermore, Star presents the key properties of infrastructure as including elements that are ubiquitous for many systems, which is why a study of infrastructure can reveal the dichotomy between collective action and formal organization to be a false one. Core archival properties, for example (such as generally accepted professional archiving principles of preserving, classifying, and cataloguing), embody the links that infrastructural systems have with conventions of practice that are learned through membership of the field that also conveys the normalization of standards. Expanding on her description of what infrastructure is, Star says it is:

- *Built on an installed base.* Infrastructure does not grow de novo; it wrestles with the inertia of the installed base and inherits strengths and limitations from that base.
- *Embeddedness.* Infrastructure is sunk into and inside of other structures, social arrangements, and technologies. People do not necessarily distinguish the several coordinated aspects of infrastructure.
- *Transparency.* Infrastructure is transparent to use, in the sense that it does not have to be reinvented each time or assembled for each task, but invisibly supports those tasks.
- *Reach or scope.* This may be either spatial or temporal – infrastructure has reach beyond a single event or one-site practice.

(Star 1999: 381–82)

These properties are arguably present in all forms of archiving. Adopting the analysis of infrastructure approach advocated by Star to understand the practices employed by the Archives Working Group becomes more useful in the context of the other properties she identifies. Infrastructure, she says:

- *Becomes visible upon breakdown.* The normally invisible quality of working infrastructure becomes visible when it breaks: the server is down, the bridge washes out, there is a power blackout. Even when there are back-up mechanisms or procedures, their existence further highlights the now-visible infrastructure.
- *Is fixed in modular increments, not all at once or globally.* Because infrastructure is big, layered, and complex, and because it means different things locally, it is never changed from above. Changes take time and negotiation, and adjustment with other aspects of the systems are involved. Nobody is really in charge of infrastructure.

(Star 1999: 381–82)

The activist archivist's argument is that the infrastructure that is relied upon, taken for granted, and normally invisible within mainstream professional practice (including conventions, standards, codes), does not meet the remit or needs of activists and the communities they represent. Their view is that the infrastructure of mainstream archiving becomes visible as a result of its breakdown, which, in the case of Occupy, provided the Archives Working Group with the opportunity – they saw it as an obligation – to explore and institute alternative organizational structures from the ground up. This position reflected the movement's argument that 'big' infrastructure (social, political, economic, human) had become visible as both the result and evidence of the system of Western capitalism breaking down, as well as justification for its preference for prefigurative political actions (Graeber 2013; Schneider 2013b: 86).

The miscommunication that emerged between the Archives Working Group and General Assembly suggests an inadequate understanding of Star's second point, that systemic change requires interaction and adjustment with and across a wider spectrum of related and cognate systems, particularly where shared communities of practice or conventions exist. In pragmatic terms, the collections and organizational modeling created by the Archives Working Group existed as an infrastructure that sat across and was integrated within a number of structures, social arrangements, and technologies. It was, for them, an enabler (system of substrates) of social and sectoral change and their key focus or topic that sought to ensure the movement's authority over the historical record of Occupy. However, the broader movement (specifically the General Assembly) perceived the collection as a barrier to the 'political' concerns of the movement and a challenge to its independence because of its ties – however critical – with institutional archival communities of practice.[15]

Regardless of any value judgment or political agenda that may be applied to the Occupy Archive, it remains significant for offering material evidence of the processes involved in the production and breakdown of other infrastructural systems to which it is connected, including: (i) traditional archiving practices, (ii) dominant governmental and corporate forms of social control critiqued by Occupy, and (iii) the approaches taken by and within the anti-institutional Occupy movement. This means that despite the Archives Working Group's own internal inconsistencies and contestations, the archive exists more than as a singular artifact of evidence that makes visible the limitations of various structures. It shows the archive as a fundamentally relational and subjective form of communication infrastructure that is uniquely suitable for expanding understandings about archiving practices in regard to the effect that interactions and interrelationships between individuals have on the production of collective memory. Focused on systems of record creation, the archive is an autoethnographic product that shows the impact of power struggles on the profession, institutions, policies, and procedures involved in the process of meaning making. It facilitates what Cook describes as being core archival work, of exploring:

> [t]he history, evolving functions, ever-changing structures, legal frameworks, devolved or regional character, and organizational cultures of institutions that create records, or similarly the biographical and psychological details of private individuals creating personal records, from letters to diaries to photographs to websites.
>
> (Cook 2011: 619)

In focusing on people and infrastructure, the archive demonstrates that the process by which an outcome is made is itself subject to a multitude of decisions and influences, most of which are invisible in the end product. The Occupy Archive captures these because of the working group's attention to collecting the experience and perspective of occupiers as the movement played out. The infrastructure-oriented approach advocated by Star is also suited to an examination of the dynamics that existed between individuals and the communities of practice that emerged around activist archiving and the Occupy Wall Street movement. In addition to offering a way to represent the products of a failure of the 'business as usual' model, the prefigurative archive provides a record of the interactions between structures during the period of crisis.[16] One member of the working group argued that the internal interactions, competition, and conflict that arose from the process-oriented horizontal organizational formats used by the movement were crucial parts of the experience of Occupy:

> The whole oddball cast of characters that was OWS, the Byzantine decision making process that prevented any decisions from being made. I['d] love for somewhere for there to be a study of how the organization and hierarchy for a non-organization and non-hierarchical entity came into being. Because from an outsider's perspective it's fascinating to see how the structure came into being ... it was a structure that was antithetical to the idea of having a structure. It drove my bureaucratic hierarchical mind crazy.
>
> (See Roberts n.d.h: 19)

Accountability: Internal activism

It can be difficult for collections to demonstrate relationships between infrastructure (often reinforced by collective action or inaction), cohorts of people, and individual agency (Message 2018a and 2018b). While it is important to understand that an archive is an infrastructure, a system (or 'means' to an end) that has its own formal and informal conventions, rules, and structures of accountability, it is also critical to recognize the Occupy Archive as an outcome of an autoethnography undertaken by the members of the Archives Working Group. Self-documentation was a key motivation for collection development, and members sought to collect materials including 'the minutes of any working group … The minutes of the GA's and any publications of any sort that were put out by any working group, or statements to the movement' (see Roberts n.d.h: 20).[17] Working group members also understood the connections between self-documentation and visibility, and the roles physical evidence can play in stakeholder management and persuasion, even where this is an internal process. It was seen as critically important for the Archives Working Group to persuade the General Assembly of the value of the historical record that they were building. It was not, in the view of the working group, enough for the movement to hold corporations and government institutions (including museums, libraries, and archives) to account. The movement had to itself be accountable for its decisions and actions.

In Star's terms, this means using the crisis generated by Occupy Wall Street to do more than criticize government and corporate tactics (by rendering them visible as a result of being broken). It also required a debate focused on the equally visible infrastructure of *the movement itself* at the points it became exposed (such as the movement's significant problems managing racism, sexism, interpersonal violence and collective forms of discrimination).[18] Recognizing that they could not possibly capture every decision, experience, and outcome produced within Liberty Plaza, Bold asked: 'What better way to make the archive accountable to the people than to make the people accountable for the archive?' Everyone in the movement, he argued, 'should be responsible for thinking historically' (quoted in Samtani 2011: 2). This approach also resonates with Star's contention that when it becomes visible upon breakdown, infrastructure 'is fixed in modular increments, not all at once or globally'. In this situation, everybody, whether they know it or not and whether or not it is acknowledged, plays a role in the changes that occur over time and through the negotiations that occur across systems (Star 1999: 82). Recognition of this broad responsibility is reflected in the second clause of the Archives Working Group's mission statement:

> Occupy Wall Street Archives Working Group … guarantees that OWS remain a transparent movement. It ensures the accountability of OWS by documenting our ideas, ideals, strategies, structure, tactics, politics, and culture of OWS and the ways it has helped reshape the political discourse in New York, the nation, and the world.
>
> (Roberts 2011a)

The working group's focus on accountability was acknowledged by some others as beneficial for the movement. Frequent discussions within the Archives Working Group also identified the value of retaining meeting notes and minutes as a way of promoting working group transparency in addition to keeping an internal record of decision-making processes for the benefit of future social movements and researchers. Despite their efforts and acknowledgments, however, a lingering but dominant perception remained that a conflict of interest existed between the Archives Working Group's contribution to transparency and its collaboration with external collecting institutions. The group continued to suffer from a generally held distrust about the association of archives with government and private institutions (including New York University when the affiliation with Tamiment Library was discussed). Debates over the role and ownership of the collections demonstrates the point that Occupy's working groups, like many of the corporations, universities, and institutions that were targeted by the movement, struggled to find a balance between managing their reputation, controlling their image, sharing their messages, and identifying and incentivizing conversations within public sphere representations (Adi 2015: 508). This was certainly the case in regard to debates about the most appropriate final location for the collections. Disagreements often revealed a deeply held distrust of private and government institutions, staff members and affiliates, and journalists, curators, and representatives from public collecting institutions.

The question of where the archives would reside in the short and long term became a divisive and contentious issue within the Archives Working Group (Evans, Perricci, and Roberts 2014; Schneider 2013b: 167–68). The problems associated with maintaining an independent archive were practical as well as ideological:

> [Bold] says he doesn't know how to have that conversation with the General Assembly. 'I can't just say, 'Do you want to ship it off to the Smithsonian?' Roberts says that this is not an option but does see the pressing need for space. 'We need somewhere to keep the stuff', she says. 'It can't be a basement. It can't be an office hall.' ... 'We might end up trying to process everything, and then eventually deeding it to Tamiment', Bold says. 'But we won't do that without the approval of the movement. The GA [General Assembly] has to decide.'
>
> (Quoted in Samtani 2011: 6)

Distrust about the Archives Working Group's reliance on external institutions to provide training, support, and expertise for their activities (and the related concern that they could not ensure accountability for the movement because they had 'sold out') was exacerbated by decisions made by the General Assembly. These coalesced specifically on the General Assembly's rejection of applications by the Archives Working Group for financial support for core activities, and on its assessment that the Archives Working Group did not qualify as a form of affective direct action.[19] Some members of the General Assembly reportedly argued that since the movement was itself ephemeral, what mattered was the occupation as it existed at that time only. They argued that retaining the material evidence was not important. This view compromised Occupy Wall Street's ability to exert control over its legacy, particularly given that other institutions were collecting as frenetically, albeit often selectively, as they could, and usually without developing relationships with occupiers (Perricci 2012; Associated Press 2011; Judkis 2011; Schuessler 2012a; Schuessler 2012b; Helmore 2015). The point was not lost on Archives Working Group members who warned that:

> There are a lot of other people recording the movement and telling its story, but we want to empower occupiers to help preserve what is being made while their story is unfolding. While some archivists aim to be dispassionate and 'objective', our intent was to be more involved in the movement and open about the inherent influence of our actions.
>
> (Evans, Perricci and Roberts 2014)

Others similarly argued that 'the last thing' they wanted was 'the historical record of OWS controlled by people who aren't in OWS' (Molenda quoted in Erde 2014: 82). If I am correct in understanding that an activist public relations interest in managing constituent relationships is designed to contribute to a self-replicating and expanding social imaginary, then the lack of support for the Archives Working Group had a negative impact on the movement's ability to further influence relationships with constituents that included the institutions that now hold and exert control over Occupy Wall Street collections.

Lack of support by the General Assembly further reflected a perception that cultural activities and events including collecting and archives are not sufficiently 'political.'[20] Distrust in the collection of images of and from Occupy (that were perhaps viewed as commodities), may have been based on the view that it was a superficial and undesirably institutionalized or consumerist activity, even public relations-like in a pejorative sense ('selling out' rather than 'capacity building'). There was no acknowledgment by the General Assembly that failure to construct an enduring archive would mean that the only remaining public representation of the movement would be held in collections not controlled (and in most cases not created) by Occupy Wall Street participants. These risks were, however, vigorously debated within the Archives Working Group. The movement's lack of interest in using traditional institutions and forms of media to co-opt or subvert mainstream news outlets or sites of representation (including museums, archives, and libraries) over the longer term contrasted with their priority for having a current impact. It meant that whilst actions perceived as being immediately 'direct' in the sense of being headline-grabbing, such as sending a high profile delegation to Tahrir Square (Roberts 2011d), were funded, applications for archival resources including banker's boxes and storage space by the Archives Working Group were rejected. The seduction of the immediate effect was evident in enthusiasm expressed for and about the media center, described in the following terms:

> Thanks to the activist habit of *ressentiment*, acquired by seeing protest after protest fail to make headlines, the Occupiers had planned for creating their own media much more than serving anyone else's. There was no place in the encampment more seemingly sophisticated and elite than the jumble of glowing laptops and indiscernible wires around the media center; visitors passed by in awe of this physical manifestation of the age of the hashtag. ... This was an important place.
>
> (Schneider 2013b: 40)

Occupy's preoccupation with maintaining its status as headline news shows that public relations *was* produced by the Occupy Wall Street movement. However, it also shows that the resulting legacy of the movement's communication efforts was not the internally produced archive (that produced, in the end, a kind of 'organizational autoethnography' (Parry and Boyle 2009) of an anti-institutional infrastructure) but the ephemeral material produced for external audiences that occupiers, by and large (and certainly many Archives Working Group members) assessed as being of low enduring significance.[21] This result is paradoxical because the life cycle of the material salvaged from the site by external collectors was generally intended to be short term but has become the primary representation of the movement. In failing to achieve internal support for the Archives Working Group's aim to preserve the historical value of the movement for future protesters by preserving internal documentation, the dominant image surviving of Occupy Wall Street are the collections made by external museums and collections.[22] In other words, what material collections remain are, ironically, the ephemeral material outputs which, despite not having been significantly valued by the movement, have been collected by and taken to 'stand in' (as indexical signifiers) for the movement as a whole by public and government institutions. The internal processes of the movement – which sought specifically to document the challenges and processes as well as the legacy of Occupy

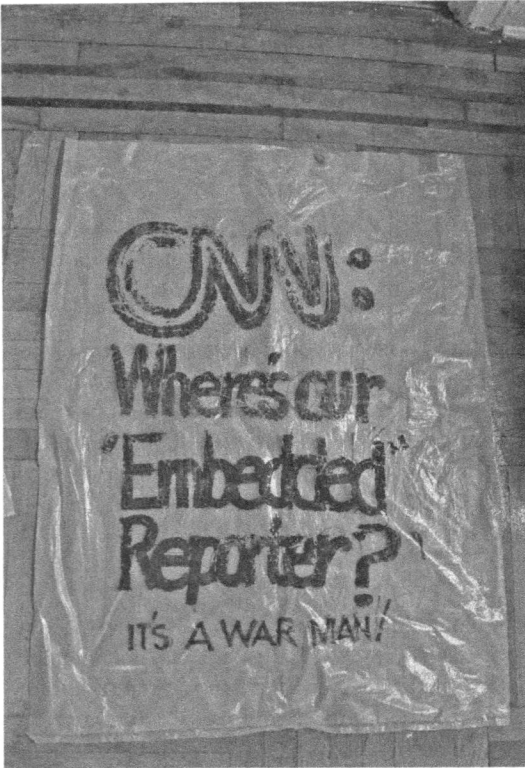

Figure 3.3 'Where's our "Embedded" Reporter?' protest sign (re-purposed foam board bag – note draft marks) from Occupy Wall Street. Unknown creator. Image from Amy Roberts' private collection (acquired by Tamiment Library in 2017).

Photograph by Kylie Message.

Wall Street for the benefit of future activists (i.e. *PR for activists not just by activists*) – are not fully represented by any public collection.

Long-term plight of Occupy Archive

Although the Archives Working Group sought to source support for an independent archive from within the movement, the task became increasingly difficult. Traditionally, archives are assembled by government institutions as a form of record keeping after the fact, most often by an archivist who is not the subject of the archive. Access to the archive is then controlled by the institution. Although the Occupy Archive was created as an autoethnographic record, in the end the working group had to hand it over to another organization to preserve, meaning they ultimately ceded control of who determines access to the material. Archives members Sian Evans, Anna Perricci, and Amy Roberts later explained:

> We wanted to ensure that the experiences that made up the Occupy movement were in fact shared, rather than locked away in a private storage locker. Ultimately, attempts to safeguard the archives outside of an institutional setting amounted to simply making them inaccessible to anyone. The collective spirit of the movement, though outside of any formal institution, will likely become dependent on one for the persistence and access to the materials. That said, some institutional settings are more appropriate than others.
>
> (Evans, Perricci, and Roberts 2014)

The working group continued to try to source support for an independent archive from within the movement (evidenced by various viewpoints articulated in response to Bold 2012a, 2012b, and 2012c), but over time moved towards identifying the Tamiment Library and Robert F. Wagner Labor Archives as their generally but by no means universally preferred repository.[23] Tamiment Library is an archive that evades easy definition because while it is *prima facie* an institutional repository like the Smithsonian Institution or the Museum of the City of New York, it is distinguished from these structurally by being owned by New York University, a private organization. The working group's preference was based on their understanding of Tamiment Library's remit to document the history of radical politics, the political left, social movements, and the labor struggle in New York City. Despite being politically aligned with the working group and sympathetic to the movement, members did not generally view the Tamiment Library as an 'activist' institution, despite the sometimes substantial contributions made by its staff members to the working group (see Roberts n.d.h: 11). They were ultimately convinced, however, by its capacity, 'good organizational structure', and resources to adequately preserve the materials, which they could not themselves even nearly match independently (Riley 2012).[24]

Extended negotiation about the transfer of materials occurred within the Archives Working Group, as well as between the working group and Tamiment Library staff members – two of whom, Chela Scott Weber, Associate Head for Archival Collections, and Michael Nash, the institution's director (who died in 2012, before the collection was acquired)[25] – had been members of the Archives Working Group. Issues to be settled included intellectual property rights, ownership of material collected from the Sanitation Department and other places following raids and seizures (where authorship could not be determined), and what the deed of gift would look like given that the donation was coming from a community archive whose membership was not standardized, and therefore had no real representation or authority to speak for the group the collection would be identified as documenting. Other less complex but no less significant priorities articulated by the Archives Working Group in relation to the transfer were expectations that the collection would be digitized in a timely manner, and made available for open access use, partly to address concerns over intellectual property, uncertain ownership of materials, and the desire not to represent or speak for others. The priority of accessibility was emphasized in negotiations. From the outset, 'the ideal was always long-term preservation paired with a consistently high level of access' (Evans, Perricci and Roberts 2014). The Archives Working Group expressed the strong preference for making the collections open to the public through open house events hosted by Tamiment Library, at which Occupy Wall Street activists and the general public could review the collection and offer comments, corrections, and annotations to the description and organization provided by the Library.[26]

The majority of the ('official') Occupy Wall Street collection was transferred to the Tamiment Library and Robert F. Wagner Labor Archives in phases, in 2013, 2014, and 2017. However, the paper-based archival documentary collections did not become available for public use until early 2018, while the signs and other three-dimensional materials including placards, textiles, and drums continue to remain unprocessed and inaccessible (Johnson 2016; Tamiment Library and Robert F. Wagner Labor Archive 2018).[27] Although I have not had space in this chapter to fully analyze the working group's relationship with Tamiment Library, the exchanges that led to that institution's acquisition of the collections exist as a third set of relationship-building strategies, the dynamics of which were also obviously influenced by both the external and internal forms of activism produced by the Archives Working Group.

Conclusion

Many people in the Occupy movement held firm opinions about the value of an independent archive and the undesirability of an institutional affiliation (where independent = good and institutional = bad). However, their preferences usually bore little correlation to properties associated with existing institutional infrastructures and specific archival typologies. Not that it would have mattered anyway, because the nature of the assemblage produced by the Archives Working Group – a collective record that combines features characteristically associated with personal records and archives (letters and diaries, Christmas cards, gift cards, delivery notices with personalized messages), as well as government archives (policies), features of institutional record keeping (meeting minutes and agendas, etc.), and materials more typically found in museum collections (signs, banners, artworks, zines, etc.) – itself confounds attempts at easy categorization.[28] Members of the Archives Working Group were constantly aware of the paradox of their attempt to create a quasi-institutional albeit independent archive that would go on to have a life beyond the movement. And while, as such, the evasion or defiance of easy categorization might have occurred as the result of accident (what happened to be collected) rather than design (what was collected as a result of discussion and planning), the activist archiving practices employed by the group worked against the possibility of being recuperated to or defined by institutions associated with the dominant historical order they sought to challenge and reconstruct.

In contrast to archives that historically have reinforced existing power relations by privileging the stories of the powerful and elite whilst excluding or marginalizing the voices of others, the Archives Working Group aimed to achieve wide participation and a diversity of voices while also recognizing the power implicit in their own role of selecting materials for the archive. Rather than establishing themselves as something further alienated by the mainstream for its 'otherness', the Archives Working Group was more interested in transforming traditional archival practices and information management systems so as to preserve and present the output of social justice movements in ways that would spur further activism beyond their immediate community (Roberts n.d.c). As they explained:

> It was this principle that guided a lot of the work we did in the OWS AWG [Occupy Wall Street Archives Working Group]. Because the group consisted of occupiers and sympathetic professionals, we embodied a mixture of archivists, activists, and archivist-activists. As such, we were careful not to impose an authoritarian, unified archival voice on the decision-making processes. Our decision-making process was consensus-based; not only did we hold weekly meetings, but we also created an open forum Google Group in which those who could not attend could voice their opinions. The discourse on the Google Group mailing list was tense at times, but it did provide a venue for people to speak freely in writing.
>
> (Evans, Perricci and Roberts 2014)

The affiliations between individual members of the Archives Working Group and external institutions and their interest in influencing mainstream archival practices may have exacerbated the distrust expressed by the movement toward the Archives Working Group. However, the networks also meant that they were already acutely familiar with the curatorial activism that occurs within even the most formal 'institutional' workplaces. Interventions made by archivists and curators such as Melder and Mayo (described in Chapter 1) and what archivist Susan Woodland from the American Jewish Historical Society has more recently called the many 'quietly activist decisions' she makes in the course of her daily work to reveal politically relevant aspects of institutional history ('NY Archives week symposium program', n.d.), are also part of the broader context in which activist archiving works today. Working group members also recognized that the act of archiving was always already based on subjective decision-making and that at no point could archival processes be assigned objectivity, regardless of the institution in which they take place. One working group member articulated his ability to make considered assessments a core part of his professional expertise: 'I am okay with the fact that appraisal decisions I make will determine the historical record, that's my responsibility as a professional' (see Roberts n.d.h: 35).[29]

One of the great strengths of the work undertaken by the Archives Working Group was their ability to keep disciplinary debates about archival practice in play with the realities and political imperatives of the movement. I know this because the archive shows it: Discussions within the group and with other parts of the movement have been documented alongside the more familiar material signifiers of the movement (signs, banners, T-shirts). The archive also evidences how adept working group members were at adjusting the demands of internal and external infrastructures around each other to accommodate the aim of contributing to both. For example, as well as maintaining commitment to social organizing and 'the work' of Occupy (participating in actions, maintaining the Liberty Plaza site and community, and so on), they remained inspired by professional debates over questions including those asked by a panel at New York Archives week:

- What is the responsibility of an archive to the community whose memory it preserves?
- How can archivists foster a sense of trust and empowerment through their many years of continuous caretaking of a local organization's or individual's historical documents?
- Whose archives? Who decides? Whose priorities take place?

('NY Archives week symposium program', n.d.)

In addition to illustrating the different communication strategies employed by the Archives Working Group for its internal and external stakeholders, the activist archiving focus of this book progresses something else, which relates back to Star's argument and makes the General Assembly's lack of support for their activities even more unfortunate. As an autoethnography of the movement and the interactions between the movement and the broader non-Occupy public (and others, including the New York City Council and New York Police Department), the archive provides a material embodiment of the most fundamental claims of Occupy. It explores what happens when organizational cultures and workplace discourses are 'transformed from vertical to horizontal, from controlling to collaborative, from stovepipes to networks, from executive fiat to internal consensus, with records created in these new milieus following these new conventions' (Cook 2011: 627–28). Although Cook examines this set changed of conditions in regard to institutional archives, they can also be applied to the anti-institutional infrastructure of the Occupy Wall Street movement evidenced by the Archives Working Group's attempt to document the decision-making processes that sought to provoke shifts in social, political, and archival practice.

Notes

1 The Archives Working Group was eligible to access a rolling provisional budget of $100 from the movement's General Assembly, which they needed to acquit before they could apply for more. Their (revised) request for $3940 to cover the basics required for short-term storage and urgent preservation was tabled and rejected at a finance meeting of the General Assembly (Roberts 2011c; 'OWS Archives Budget Proposal' 2012).

2 Other materials included protester's chains and a padlock, a large blue foam finger with the phrase 'Tax Dodgers 1%' (parody of the LA Dodgers fan signs waved at baseball games), and a kitchen donation box (Tamiment Library and Robert F. Wagner Labor Archive 2018).

3 The Google group was accessed by members through subscription. It is now archived and not publicly accessible. I was granted membership by Roberts to review the archive's contents. Many of the discussion threads were also collected at http://www.nycga.net/groups/the-occupy-wallstreet-archives but these are no longer live. Similarly, the minutes and documents relating to the operations and decisions of the NYCGA were online for many years at http://www.nycga.net/ but the link became dead mid-2017.

4 As explained in Chapter 1, the term 'OWS archives' is an umbrella phrase that confounds traditional distinctions about which materials should go into museums and archives respectively. It includes the collections that have been used for the case study in this book; primarily those at Tamiment Library that I have referred to as the 'Occupy Archive' (including the previously private collection of signs analyzed in Chapter 2), and the born digital Google group forum. However, it extends to include other collections, such as those held by other institutions, and also includes the digital collections and oral history collections that I have excluded from my analysis. The term also recognizes that the status and ownership of collections themselves continue to change and affect how they

are formally regarded (evidenced by the incremental accessioning of materials into Tamiment Library between 2012 and 2017).

5 The 'NO MORE BUSINESS AS USUAL' sign reproduced in Figure 3.1 captures the feeling of many in the Occupy movement who

> claimed the right of we the people to create a world that works for the 99% ... The shame many of us felt when we couldn't find a job, pay down our debts, or keep our home is being replaced by a political awakening.
>
> (van Gelder 2011a: 2)

6 Cook (2011: 623) argues that 'archivists need an intellectual history of their own profession, from the inside out *and* the outside in'.

7 Discomfort with attempts to glamorize activism was usefully expressed in the following way by a discussion between members of the Occupy Museums group:

> We believe that institutions promoting a cult of celebrity, unfair labor practices, extreme commodification of art, and which trivialize or glamorize political struggle and protest are only the logical outcome of an entire culture stolen from the people by the 1%.

The concern was that glamorization was a process of depoliticization (Noah Fischer, 'Occupy Museums Update', Arts and Culture, http://www.nycga.net/group-documents/occupy-museums-update/, link no longer live). Also see the Editorial Note printed in the first issue of the *Occupied Wall Street Journal* (2011: n.p.):

> Barricaded in by steel pens, surrounded by a thousand cops and NYPD helicopters above, we saw our power reflected in their need to control us. But just as this is our movement, it is our narrative too. The exhausted political machines and their PR slicks are already seeking leaders to elevate, messages to claim. Talking points to move on. They, more than anyone, will attempt to seize and shape this moment.

8 The intention for continuing a process of re-use and re-cycling materials was also adopted as a goal by Interference Archives, where a concept called 'preservation through use' is employed (Sellie *et al.* 2015: 461). One of the co-founders of Interference Archive, Josh McPhee, was also associated with the Occupy Wall Street Archives Working Group. Of the work done at Interference Archive, he says:

> Preserving the material is only meaningful if it continues to be used. ... 'It was produced with the intention of distribution. The ideas are there to be engaged with and to be brought back out in the world. Hopefully there's an effect and new things come into the archive'.
>
> (Quoted in Helmore 2015)

9 Phrase taken from a sign quoted in Solnit (2011: 80).

10 Perhaps as consistent with my counting and classifying-based audit of materials, fonts, capitalization and the like in Chapter 2, Star says that 'many aspects of infrastructure are singularly unexciting. They appear as lists of numbers and technical specifications, or as hidden mechanisms subtending those processes more familiar to social scientists. It takes some digging to unearth the dramas inherent in system design creating, to restore narrative to what appears to be dead lists' (Star 1999: 377).

11 Taussig (2013: 20).

12 Presenting a synoptic overview of the benefits of ethnographic studies, Tammar Zilber quotes Watson (2011) who argues that they

> may yield indispensable insights about the social dynamics of the field, insights that cannot be discovered and analyzed otherwise. Ethnography allows us to study the 'extraordinary-in-the-ordinary' (Ybema et al. 2009: 2), the social processes involved in constructing and allowing for the everyday ordinary lived experiences of people within organizational and inter-organizational spheres. It also allows learning about 'what "actually happens" or about "how things work"'.
>
> (Zilber 2014: 97)

It enables thus a focus on the hidden, the less visible and less explicit dimensions of organizational or inter-organizational life, including emotions and power relations, thus highlighting 'the interplay between actors (whether individual or collective) and context (Yanow et al. 2012)' (quoted in Zilber 2014: 97). Organizational autoethnography extends this focus by illuminating relationships between individuals and organizations to examine culture as it is practiced and understood within institutional and organizational settings (Parry and Boyle 2009).

13 The use of embedded ethnographic methods to collect data about Occupy for subsequent interpretation was frequently employed by a range of researchers. For example, Schneider recommended ethnographic methods for engaging in the process of 'the spectacle', saying they provided him with a strategy for how to tell 'the kinds of stories I needed to learn how to tell' (Schneider 2013b: 8; also see Taussig 2013).

14 Cook and Stoler both criticize historians for 'mining' archives for information rather than engaging with questions about how and why they have been created (and by whom). Cook argues that:

> Historians and archivists approach the documentary past differently, as they consider, respectively, the 'archive' (singular) and 'archives' (plural). The former focuses on issues of power, memory, and identity centered upon the initial inscription of a document (or series of documents). The latter concentrates on the subsequent history of documents over time, including the many interventions by archivists (and others) that transform (and change) that original archive into archives.
>
> (Cook 2011: 600)

I have elected to use both singular and plural forms of 'archive', as I have done in previous chapters with 'collection' and collections'.

15 The working group's embeddedness in a network of activity and tool-based infrastructures that connected the Occupy movement and the archiving sector curtailed their work as much as it offered an opportunity to extend the movement's political principles. This was primarily because the Occupy Wall Street General Assembly perceived the archive as a barrier of sorts – a reminder of the mainstream infrastructure and order they wanted to challenge and replace with an altogether new system of economic, social and political equity.

16 Perhaps adding weight to the argument in Micah White's book, *The End of Protest*, where he argued that Occupy Wall Street, a movement he claims co-creation rights over, 'broke' protest, and that activism is, like the system it sought to disrupt, 'in crisis' (White 2016: 35).

17 This working group member went on to add: 'The minutes of any working group would be really interesting to have. The minutes of the GAs and any publications of any sort that were put out by any working group, Or kind of statements to the movement. Anything. … And if we want to have a record of this then it's going to be five years, then a paper printout from Tamiment probably still will be in existence, but I can't guarantee that any of those website will still be up', which, incidentally, is a reasonable reflection of what ended up happening (see Roberts n.d.h: 20).

18 Records of internal discussions include 'Minutes from meeting with Tamiment' (2012). Extensive debate over the responsibility for thinking politically as well as historically – in *personal* terms – also occurred within the group and across the movement, which advocated for a leaderless horizontal form of organization. Criticisms about the way the movement reproduced social and political inequalities based on sexual preference and race as well as gender and class were widely articulated, as were concerns that particular individuals or cliques gained dominance, greater authority or representation in decision-making processes regardless of the movement's ostensible commitment to consensus (Ashraf 2011; McVeigh 2011).

19 The lack of support for the actions of the Archives Working Group can be summarized by two decisions made by the General Assembly on November 9 and 10, 2011. First, the rejection of their budget request (Roberts 2011d; Minutes from Occupy Wall Street General Assembly [11/11/2011, at www.nycga. net/2011/11/10/nycga-minutes-11102011/#more-3183, link no longer live]). Second, their application (tabled the second day) to move from a Working Group to an Operational Group, defined as groups that were concerned with direct action implementation in contrast with other support-focused subsidiary groups that were ineligible for funding, was rejected after a motion was moved against the Archives Working Group. 'About eight' peer working groups were reported as having voted against Archives becoming an Operational group (Roberts 2011d; OWS Structure Working Group 2011; Molenda 2011b). About the Occupy Archives' request for budget from Occupy Wall Street General Assembly (01/15/2012, at www.nycga.net/2012/01/1132012-archives-budget/, link no longer live), one contributor to the discussion thread stated: 'This sounds like what we are fighting!! I'm sure the occupier that is sleeping on the subway will appreciate that their sign is in a climate controlled room … OWS does not need a museum'.

20 Robust debate over what constituted direct action occurred during and after the Zuccotti Park occupation, including about the role (and funding) of art and 'outreach' activities. One participant wrote: 'According to our wiki, here's

the definition: an agreed upon event that has a noted intent, strategy, outcome, and contingency plan(s); http://wiki.occupy.net/wiki/OWS_Comprehensive_ Glossary#A' (02/25/2012, http://www.nycga.net/2012/03/logo-proposal/; but discussion thread lasts all through February–March 2012; see for example http://www.nycga.net/2012/02/end-the-spending-freeze/; http://www.nycga. net/2012/03/proposal-for-printing-may-day-poster/, links no longer live). This chapter aims to challenge distinctions between culture and politics by demonstrating the relationship between cultural collections, public relations, activism, and 'the political dimensions of struggle and change' (L'Etang 2016: 207; also 'Organizational documents – Archives working group 2011–2012').

21 Occupy Wall Street Archives Working Group members also articulated the view that the material collection was only one element of the record and only important in the context of oral histories and other forms of recording (including born digital resources). Perhaps influenced by the movement's preference for and investment in digital media forms of communication, some members were unenthusiastic about the collection of posters and ephemera (Roberts n.d.j). There was also a broader ideological preference across the movement for the 'occupation of a physical space as an ongoing symbolic critique rather than as focused industrial demand' (Erde 2014: 77).

22 The internal processes of Occupy Wall Street are increasingly becoming subject to critical reflection (Schneider 2013a; White 2016) but the material documentation records of the movement are only starting to become accessible to researchers, with much content still inaccessible (Tamiment Library and Robert F. Wagner Labor Archive 2018).

23 The question of where the archives would reside in the short and long term was a divisive and contentious issue within the working group (Evans, Perricci, and Roberts 2014; Bold quoted in Samtani 2011: 6). In response to eventual transfer of materials to Tamiment Library, one working group member said:

> Was there another option? Really, a credible other option? I'm not sure there was. The people still willing to work on the collection did not have the time, resources (financial), or space to truly deal with the collection, and the various non-traditional radical spaces out there (Interference Archives for example) were not going to be able to handle a collection of its size. Tamiment is the main archive for radical movements in the US, and while it is held by NYU (a private university) I am ultimately rather pleased to think that materials I was involved with are sharing an archive with the papers of Eugene Debs and the Abraham Lincoln brigade. Tamiment tells the story of radical movements in the US, OWS is part of that story.
>
> (See Roberts n.d.h: 25)

24 Tamiment Library and Robert F. Wagner Labor Archives mission statement at https://library.nyu.edu/locations/the-tamiment-library-robert-f-wagner-labor-archives/. Also see Cary (2013: 18), who notes that what had previously been the Tamiment Institute donated its collection to New York University in 1963 when its capacity to remain independent became tenuous after its tax-exempt status was revoked.

25 A special issue of *American Communist History* (2013) dedicated to Michael Nash includes broader historical context about the Tamiment Library.

26 A representative of Tamiment Library said that once the collections were processed, the institution could host open house events in which Occupy Wall Street activists and the general public could review the collection and offer comments, corrections and annotations to the description and organization provided by Tamiment Library (reported in Bold 2012c).

27 The collection was unprocessed and unavailable for many years. Requests by researchers and the collection's donor (myself and Roberts) to access the collection were refused, as were offers to process its materials for the institution throughout 2016 and 2017 (Johnson 2016; Message 2017a; Message 2017b). The collection was made partially accessible in January 2018 (Tamiment Library and Robert F. Wagner Labor Archive 2018).

28 John Erde argues that collections of Occupy materials constitute a community archive because, '[i]n common with other community archives, the OWSAG [Occupy Wall Street Archives Group] collects many "ephemeral" materials that do not conform to traditional definitions of "records" or "archives".' He gives the pizza box signs as an example (Erde 2014: 80). He also says there are no fixed and universally accepted definitions of the terms 'community', 'archive', and 'community archive', and so recommends adopting the definition that 'A community, in short, is any group of people who come together and present themselves as such, and a "community archive" is the product of their attempts to document the history of their commonality' (from Flinn, Stevens, and Shepherd 2009: 75).

29 This working group member's account of his professional responsibilities echo Stoler's observation that:

> As archivists are the first to note, to understand an archive one needs to understand the institutions that it served. What subjects are cross-referenced, what parts are re-written, what quotations are cited, not only tell us about how decisions are rendered, but how colonial histories are written and remade.
>
> (Stoler 2002: 107; also Greene 2013; Jimerson 2013)

This changes everything[1]

'Whatever happens next', argued van Gelder in 2011, 'Occupy Wall Street has already accomplished something that changes everything' (van Gelder 2011a: 11). The 'everything' that had been changed was, she said, the 'the national conversation' around democracy, systems of governance, and economic justice. To indicate the extent of this change, she directly invoked the impact the movement had exerted on public history: 'The 99% are no longer sitting on the sidelines of history – we are making history' (van Gelder 2011a: 12). However, while there is little doubt of the impact that the images of protest signs had on the national – and global – public imaginary, questions about the movement's broader support for historical preservation of the material records that constitute the self-authored legacy of Occupy Wall Street remain open and alive to this day.

This book has considered these questions through a case study of the material legacy of Occupy Wall Street. I approached this task by providing an account of how an object-based collection was produced throughout the movement. I then examined the record of interactions between the Occupy Archives Working Group and other participants of Occupy (via General Assembly interactions and decisions) to analyze the ambivalent support provided by the broader movement to the activities of the working group and the archive it produced in the name of the movement. The book has aimed to move between analysis of the working group's contribution to the Occupy Wall Street movement and the broader context of a prefigurative social movement on the one hand, and assessment, on the other hand, of the practices of contemporary cause-based collecting and activist archiving that were undertaken.

This book presents the Occupy Archive as its primary field of reference: The archive was my 'field-site'. I took this approach because the archive was created to represent the movement publicly, and because I wanted the book to make a case for the contribution that autoethnographic records of social reform movements can make to curatorial activism as it has been described

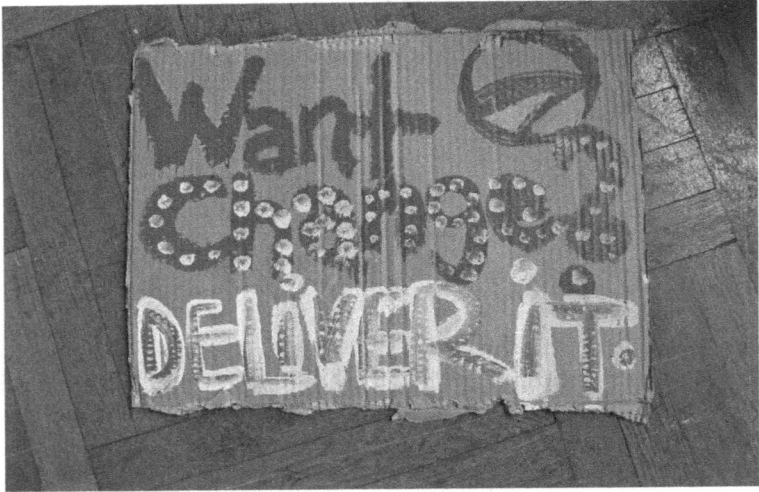

Figure E.1 Protest sign from Occupy Wall Street with Obama reference. Unknown creator. Image from Amy Roberts' private collection (acquired by Tamiment Library in 2017).

Photograph by Kylie Message.

throughout *The Disobedient Museum* trilogy. Contra the sometimes hostile responses expressed by others in the movement during and after the period of encampment at Zuccotti Park, the working group's actions and accounts created a public narrative for the movement that would otherwise simply not exist. As such, it felt relevant and urgent to present the archive as core evidence missing from van Gelder's claim that the 99% had made a contribution to public and political history.

Collecting Activism, Archiving Occupy Wall Street is the third and final book in a trilogy that has sought to model a process of politically engaged and affective scholarship to influence ways in which scholars from museum studies and affiliated fields address their topic as subjects rather than sources. It has sought to encapsulate and apply the key theoretical questions and concerns of the Museums in Focus series in relation to the agendas and activities of the Occupy Wall Street movement. Arguing that what David Graeber calls 'insurgent writing' (Graeber 2008 in Message 2018a: 54) occurs when theory and practice come together, the overarching approach employed by the trilogy has been to investigate the role of museums and collections as sites of structure and resistance in the context of contemporary activism, from three different angles. Book 1, *The Disobedient Museum: Writing at the Edge* (Message 2018a), presents a critical examination of structures of writing about museums and activism. Ideas-based and focused on disciplinary practices, it is theoretical/conceptual, and written primarily for an academic readership of museum studies and cultural studies scholars. This is the core general readership of all three books, but the next two books seek also to attract more targeted audiences. Book 2, *Museums and Racism* (Message 2018b), is focused on the structures of governance and the possibilities for and practices of internal institutional disobedience. A case study analysis of institutions and government policy, its additional readership is museum professionals and policymakers. Book 3, *Collecting Activism, Archiving Occupy Wall Street,* focuses on the experience, structure, and documentation of resistance from the perspective of the anti-institutional reform movement of Occupy Wall Street as it is represented in the Occupy Archive. It aims to make a contribution to public histories and practices of contemporary cause-based collecting.

Collecting Activism, Archiving Occupy Wall Street complements the previous books by drawing together the examination of sociopolitical context presented in Book 1 (attention to 'breadth') with analysis of the internal institutional perspective/response to activism and social reform movements (insistence on 'depth') presented in Book 2. Overlaying breadth and depth, it offers a final culminating case study focused on the perspective of activist collecting, the context in which collectors work, and the collections and archives they create. I identify the practices of the Occupy Archives Working Group as critical actions that extend and illuminate many of the theoretical and methodological discussions examined in the previous two books, particularly the contention that resistance occurs most effectively through a process of disruption that works within and across relevant infrastructures (be they institutional or anti-institutional). Whilst this final book provides a continuum of previous narratives and some summative comments, my primary intention is that it offer a stand-alone case study. It does not substantively revisit the theoretical material and framing discussions occurring in previous books. Readers interested in further theorization about the interaction between museum theory and practice, insurgent writing, and social and academic activism are directed to *The Disobedient Museum* (Message 2018a).

An additional focus for this book was an examination of the possibilities and limitations of archival research. Following Stoler (2010), I sought to engage with the archive as a primary subject rather than as a secondary context. I elected to examine the archive according to its self-declared mission to provide a self-representational record of the movement, as a 'place' of research. I determined to contain my research to the archive as much as possible, to clearly position it as a test case for examining *what* it said on behalf of its makers and *how* it spoke. This approach was particularly relevant to the Occupy Archive because of its dual focus on objects produced by occupiers and documentation about the working group's decisions in the context of debates occurring within the broader movement. The approach also allowed me to engage with and depict the benefits and challenges of employing collections analysis as a central investigative approach.

While my approach allowed me to access a partial inside view, I never saw or aspired to see my engagement with the archive as an invitation or opportunity to become an insider. I wanted instead to represent the actions and opinions of working group members in the words and language included in the archives. Limitations exist in taking this approach, and part of my aim for *The Disobedient Museum* trilogy was to create an experimental platform to explore methodologies that may or may not work in order to *show how and why* limitations occur or exist. As is the case with any collection, there are also obviously biases and gaps within the archive that are also replicated here. My approach did not include substantive interviewing of participants, because I wanted to engage with the subjective narratives of Occupy as they were constructed and developed *at the time* by participants. I was also conscious of acknowledging and giving a platform to the rich collections that have been assembled in this unique archive, which continue to remain almost completely inaccessible. It was important, I felt, for them to be allowed to speak.

Furthermore and finally, I sought, following Stoler, to frame my project around a study of process: 'the task is less to distinguish fiction from fact than to track the production and consumption of those "facts" themselves' (Stoler 2002: 91). This emphasis is evident in the archive, which embodies the preference of Occupy Wall Street as a prefigurative movement on being 'means' or process driven rather than focused on 'ends' or outcomes. It is embodied practically as well as conceptually, such that even the collections that were acquired by Tamiment Library as late as 2017 retained the order in which the materials were collected and came into the Archive.

In the final instance, *Collecting Activism, Archiving Occupy Wall Street* explores activist collecting in relation to the case study of Occupy Wall Street. Specifically concerned with the experience of participating in, documenting, and analyzing protest and reform movements, the book investigates what contribution a dual study of the material culture of dissent and the production of a collection hosting the material culture of dissent might offer to a range of disciplines and practices. Its key aim is to examine if and how such a collection can test theoretical propositions around the tactics of activism from archival and museological perspectives. It presents the collection and the process of creating the collection (its two subjects) as lenses through which to examine the sociology of protest and reform movements to represent the experience of people involved in political, social, and

cultural critique, including those working within proto-institutional structures and perspectives. Case study focused, it models strategies for 'activating' historical archives and collections-based data, and for engaging with
autoethnography and contemporary cause-based collecting to represent and
analyze the material residue of protest and reform movements.

Note

1 Van Gelder (2011a): 1.

Bibliography

Activist Archivists (2012) 'Why Archive?' October 19. Online at http://activist-archivists.org/wp/?p=994. Accessed August 4, 2018.

Adams, Tony E., Holman Jones, Stacy, and Ellis, Carolyn (2015) *Autoethnography: Understanding Qualitative Research*, New York, NY: Oxford University Press.

Adi, Ana (2015) 'Occupy PR: An Analysis of Online Media Communications of Occupy Wall Street and Occupy London', *Public Relations Review* 41: 508–14.

American Communist History (2013) 'Special Issue Dedicated to Michael Nash', *American Communist History* 12(1): 39–40.

Appadurai, Arjun and Breckenridge, Carol (1992) 'Museums Are Good to Think: Heritage on View in India', in I. Karp, C. Mullen Kreamer, and S. D. Lavine (eds.) *Museums and Communities: The Politics of Public Culture*, Washington, DC and London: Smithsonian Institution Press, pp. 34–55.

Archivists Watch (2011) 'Occupy Wall Street Library and Archives', November 18. Online at http://thearchivistswatch.wordpress.com/2011/11/18/occupy-wall-street-library-and-archives. Accessed August 4, 2018.

Ashraf, Hena (2011) 'Claiming Space for Diversity at Occupy Wall Street', in S. van Gelder (ed.) *This Changes Everything: Occupy Wall Street and the 99% Movement*, San Francisco, CA: Berrett-Koehler Publishers, Inc., pp. 33–35.

Associated Press (2011) 'Occupy Wall Street Becomes Highly Collectible', *Mercury News*, December 24. Online at https://www.mercurynews.com/2011/12/24/occupy-wall-street-becomes-highly-collectible/. Accessed February 21, 2018.

Cleveland, A. T. (2011) 'Data Mining for Instant History: Documenting the Occupy Protests', *Economist*, December 7. Online at https://www.economist.com/prospero/2011/12/07/data-mining-for-instant-history?fsrc=scn/tw/te/bl/dataminingforinstanthistory. Accessed August 4, 2018.

Atkinson, Ron (1992) 'In Defense of Relativism', *Journal of Academic Librarianship* 17(6): 353–54.

Barber, Benjamin R. (2012) 'Occupy Wall Street – "We Are What Democracy Looks Like!"', *Huffington Post*, January 7. Online at https://www.huffingtonpost.com/benjamin-r-barber/occupy-wall-street---we-a_b_1079723.html. Accessed January 16, 2019.

Bateson, Gregory (1978) *Steps to an Ecology of Mind*, New York, NY: Ballantine.

Bauer, A. J. (2012) 'The Question of Infrastructure: An Interview with Michael Ralph', *Social Text Collective*, Special Issue: 'Is This What Democracy Looks Like?' December 9. Online at https://what-democracy-looks-like.org/the-question-of-infrastructure-an-interview-with-michael-ralph/. Accessed January 16, 2019.

Baumgarten, Britta, Priska, Daphi, and Ullrich, Peter (eds.) (2014) *Conceptualizing Culture in Social Movement Research*, New York, NY: Palgrave Macmillan.

Beeston, Laura (2011) 'The Ballerina and the Bull: Adbusters' Micah White on "The Last Great Social Movement"', *The Link*, October 11. Online at https://thelinknewspaper.ca/article/the-ballerina-and-the-bull. Accessed February 21, 2018.

Beirut, Michael (2012) 'The Poster that Launched a Movement (or Not)', *Observatory*, April 30. Online at https://designobserver.com/feature/the-poster-that-launched-a-movement-or-not/32588. Accessed January 16, 2019.

Benedetto, Ida (2011) 'The Visual Politics of Occupy Wall Street', *Reading the Pictures*, November 21. Online at https://www.readingthepictures.org/2011/11/bagnewssalon-occupy-wall-street/. Accessed February 21, 2018.

Bennett, Tony (1995) *The Birth of the Museum: History, Theory, Politics*, London and New York, NY: Routledge.

Besser, Howard (2012) 'Archiving Large Swaths of User-Contributed Digital Content: Lessons from Archiving the Occupy Movement', Presentation Delivered at the *Spring 2012 Conference of the Coalition for Networked Information*, April 2. Online at http://www.cni.org/topics/digital-curation/archiving-large-swaths-of-user-contributed-digital-content. Accessed August 4, 2018.

Bold, Jeremy [Jez] (2011a) 'Archives Email+Phone #, Call for Contact Persons, and Transparency concerns', Discussion Post, Occupy Wall Street Archives Google Groups Forum, October 25. Online at https://groups.google.com/forum/#!topic/ows-archives/SqPUx9JdEs0. Accessed August 8, 2018.

Bold, Jeremy [Jez] (2011b) 'Minutes 2011/12/12', Discussion Post, Occupy Wall Street Archives Google Groups Forum, December 12. Online at https://groups.google.com/forum/#!topic/ows-archives/XSHLhqhpp6U. Accessed August 8, 2018.

Bold, Jeremy [Jez] (2012a) 'The OWS Archives: What Does It Seem Like We Can Agree On?' Discussion Post, Occupy Wall Street Archives Google Groups Forum, June 29. Online at https://groups.google.com/forum/#!topic/ows-archives/C1ItoisYAp8. Accessed August 8, 2018.

Bold, Jeremy [Jez] (2012b) '[DRAFT] Event Announcement: Who Will Keep the Archives of Occupy Wall Street?' Discussion Post and Attachment, Occupy Wall Street Archives Google Group Forum, August 3. Online at https://groups.google.com/forum/#!topic/ows-archives/PQrXpYrzKQE. Accessed August 8, 2018.

Bold, Jeremy [Jez] (2012c) 'Minutes from 2012. AUG.2 Meeting @ Tamiment', Discussion Post and Attachment, Occupy Wall Street Archives Google Group Forum, August 3. Online at https://groups.google.com/forum/#!topic/ows-archives/C0aKX7dH3L0. Accessed August 8, 2018.

Bouma, Gary (1998) 'Distinguishing Institutions and Organisations in Social Change', *Journal of Sociology* 34(3): 232–45.

Brennan, Sheila (2012) 'Looking at the #Occupy Archive', *Lot 49*, January 23. Online at http://www.lotfortynine.org/2012/01/looking-at-the-occupy-archive. Accessed August 4, 2018.

Broadbent, Jeffrey P. (2018) 'Conceptualizing Culture in Social Movement Research', *Social Movement Studies* 17(6): 749–51.

Brookfield Properties (2006) 'Brookfield Properties Re-Opens Lower Manhattan Park Following $8 Million Renovation' (Press Release), June 1. Online at http://www.marketwired.com/press-release/brookfield-properties-re-opens-lower-manhattan-park-following-8-million-renovation-tsx-bpo-597554.htm. Accessed August 4, 2018.

Brown, Steve, Frederick, Ursula, and Clarke, Anne (2015) 'Encounter, Engagement, and Object Stories', in S. Brown, A. Clarke, and U. Frederick (eds.) *Object Stories: Artifacts and Archaeologists*, Walnut Creek, CA: Left Coast Press, pp. 13–28.

Butler, Judith (2017) 'Reflections on Trump', *Hot Spots, Cultural Anthropology Website*, January 18. Online at https://culanth.org/fieldsights/1032-reflections-ontrump. Accessed February 21, 2018.

Cary, Larry (2013) '35-Year History of the Robert F. Wagner Labor Archives', *American Communist History* 12(1): 17–29.

Caswell, Michelle (2010) 'Hannah Arendt's World: Bureaucracy, Documentation, and Banal Evil', *Archivaria* 70(Fall): 1–25.

Chang, Heewon (2008) *Autoethnography as Method*, Walnut Creek, CA: Left Coast Press.

Chapin, Emily (2017) 'Collections Process', Email to Kylie Message, July 19, 2017.

Chesters, Graeme (2012) 'Social Movements and the Ethics of Knowledge Production', *Social Movement Studies* 11(2): 145–60.

Clark, Barbara (2016) 'Re: Collections Query – Occupy Wall Street', Email to Kylie Message, October 27, 2016.

Clegg, Stewart R. and Bailey, James R. (eds.) (2008) *International Encyclopedia of Organization Studies*, London: Sage.

Clifford, James (1986) 'Introduction: Partial Truths', in J. Clifford and G. E. Marcus (eds.) *Writing Culture: The Poetics and Politics of Ethnography*, Berkeley and Los Angeles, CA: University of California Press, pp. 1–26.

Clifford, James (1997) *Routes: Travel and Translation in the Late Twentieth Century*, Cambridge, MA: Harvard University Press.

Cohen-Stratyner, Barbara (2017) 'What Democracy Looks Like: Crowd-Collecting Protest Materials', *Museums & Social Issues* 12(2): 83–91.

Cook, Terry (2011) 'The Archive(s) Is a Foreign Country: Historians, Archivists, and the Changing Archival Landscape', *American Archivist* 74(2): 600–32.

Cook, Terry and Schwartz, Joan M. (2002) 'Archives, Records, and Power: From (Postmodern) Theory to (Archival) Performance', *Archival Science* 2: 171–85.

Coombs, Timothy W. and Holladay, Sherry J. (2010) *PR Strategy and Application: Managing Influence*, Malden, MA: Wiley Blackwell Publishing.

Coombs, Timothy W. and Holladay, Sherry J. (2012) 'Privileging An Activist vs. A Corporate View of Public Relations History in the U. S.', *Public Relations Review* 38: 347–53.

Culture and Organization (2007) 'Special Issue: Organizational Autoethnography', *Culture and Organization* 13(3): 185–90.

Dean, Michelle (2001) 'The Struggle for The Occupy Wall Street Archives', *Awl*, December 21. Online at https://www.theawl.com/2011/12/the-struggle-for-the-occupy-wall-street-archives/. Accessed August 17, 2016.

Del Signore, John (2011) 'Museums Archiving Occupy Wall Street: Historical Preservation Or "Taxpayer-Funded Hoarding"?' *Gothamist*, December 26. Online at http://gothamist.com/2011/12/26/occupy_wall_street_the_museum_exhib.php. Accessed August 4, 2018.

Dudley, Sandra (ed.) (2012) *Museum Objects: Experiencing the Properties of Things*, London: Routledge.

Dunlap, David W. (2006) 'Back at His Bench Downtown, Having Survived 9/11', *New York Times*, June 1. Online at https://www.nytimes.com/2006/06/01/nyregion/01cnd-park.html. Accessed August 4, 2018.

Edmundson, Anna (2015) 'Curating in the Postdigital Age', *M/C Journal* 18(4), August. Online at http://www.journal.media-culture.org.au/index.php/mcjournal/article/view/1016. Accessed March 25, 2019.

Ellis, Carolyn, Adams, Tony E., and Bochner, Arthur P. (2010) 'Autoethnography: An Overview', *Forum Qualitative Sozialforschung/Forum: Qualitative Social Research* 12(1). Online at http://nbn-resolving.de/urn:nbn:de:0114-fqs1101108. Accessed August 4, 2018.

Erde, John (2014) 'Constructing Archives of the Occupy Movement', *Archives and Records* 35(2): 77–92.

Eschle, Catherine (2018) 'Troubling Stories of the End of Occupy: Feminist Narratives of Betrayal at Occupy Glasgow', *Social Movement Studies* 17(5): 524–40.

L'Etang, Jacquie (2016) 'Public Relations, Activism and Social Movements: Critical Perspectives', *Public Relations Inquiry* 5(3): 207–11.

Evans, Sian, Perricci, Anna, and Roberts, Amy (2014) '"Why Archive?" and Other Important Questions Asked by Occupiers', in M. Morrone (ed.) *Informed Agitation: Library and Information Skills in Social Justice Movements and Beyond*, Sacramento, CA: Library Juice Press, pp. 289–306. Online at https://academiccommons.columbia.edu/doi/10.7916/D80R9MGR. Accessed January 17, 2017.

Fales Library and Special Collections (2017) Guide to the Guerrilla Girls Archive 1985–2010 MSS.274, July 5, New York, NY: Fales Library and Special Collections, Elmer Bobst Library. Online at http://dlib.nyu.edu/findingaids/html/fales/ggirls/ggirls.html. Accessed June 21, 2018.

Ferro, Shane (2011) 'The Smithsonian and New-York Historical Society Race to Preserve Occupy Wall Street's Art and Artifacts', *ArtInfo*, October 20. Online at http://www.artinfo.com/news/story/38922/the-smithsonian-and-new-york-historical-society-race-to-preserve-occupy-wall-streets-art-and-artifacts. Accessed August 4, 2018.

Flamini, Roland (2011) 'Memorabilia: Cultural Timepieces or Archival Ephemera?' *Washington Times*, November 30. Online at https://www.washingtontimes.com/news/2011/nov/30/national-museum-of-american-history-collects-occup/. Accessed August 4, 2018.

Flinn, Andrew and Alexander, Ben (eds.) (2015) 'Special Issue Archiving Activism and Activist Archiving', *Archival Science* 15(4): 329–35.

Flinn, Andrew, Stevens, Mary, and Shepherd, Elizabeth (2009) '"Whose Memories, Whose Archives?" Independent Community Archives, Autonomy and the Mainstream', *Archival Science* 9(1–2): 71–86.

Gajdukowa, Katharina (2002) 'Review Essay: Change of Paradigms in the Research on Social Movements', *Forum: Qualitative Social Research* 3(4). Online at http://www.qualitative-research.net/index.php/fqs/article/view/807/1751. Accessed November 5, 2018.

Gardner, James B. (2015) 'From Idiosyncratic to Integrated: Strategic Planning for Collections', in C. McCarthy (ed.) *Museum Practice*, Chichester: Wiley Blackwell, pp. 203–21.

Gardner, James B. (2016) 'Collecting a National Tragedy: The National Museum of American History and September 11', in M. J. Arnoldi (ed.) *Engaging Smithsonian Objects through Science, History and the* Arts, Washington, DC: Smithsonian Institution Scholarly Press, pp. 279–91.

van Gelder, Sarah (2011a) 'Introduction: How Occupy Wall Street Changes Everything', in S. van Gelder (ed.) *This Changes Everything*: *Occupy Wall Street and the 99% Movement*, San Francisco, CA: Berrett-Koehler Publishers, Inc., pp. 1–13.

van Gelder, Sarah (2011b) '10 Ways to Support the Movement', in S. van Gelder (ed.) *This Changes Everything*: *Occupy Wall Street and the 99% Movement*, San Francisco, CA: Berrett-Koehler Publishers, Inc., pp. 83–84.

Gimein, Mark (2011) '60 Wall Street: The Real Headquarters of OWS', *Bloomberg Business Week*, October. Online at https://www.bloomberg.com/businessweek/finance/occupy-wall-street/archives/2011/10/60_wall_street_the_real_head quarters_of_ows.html. Link no longer live. Accessed February 7, 2012.

Goldie, Peter (2012) *The Mess Inside: Narrative, Emotion, and the Mind*, Oxford: Oxford University Press.

Gopnik, Blake (2011) 'Occupy Wall Street Protest's Deliberate Use of Messy Signs', *Daily Beast*, November 3. Online at https://www.thedailybeast.com/occupy-wall-street-protests-deliberate-use-of-messy-signs?ref=scroll. Accessed August 4, 2018.

Graeber, David (2011) 'Enacting the Impossible: On Consensus and Decision Making', *Occupied Wall Street Journal* 3: n.p., October 22.

Graeber, David (2013) *The Democracy Project: A History, a Crisis, a Movement*, London: Penguin Books.

Greene, Mark A. (2013) 'A Critique of Social Justice as an Archival Imperative: What Is It We're Doing That's All That Important?' *American Archivist* 76(2): 302–34.

'Group Registration Form' (n.d.) Occupy Wall Street Archives Working Group Records, TAM 630, Box 2, Folder 2.4, 'Feb 2012' Notebook, Organizational Documents – Archives Working Group 2011–2012, New York, NY: Tamiment Library/Robert F. Wagner Labor Archives, New York University.

Hall, Stuart (2001) 'Constituting the Archive', *Third Text* 15(54): 89–92.

Haenfler, Ross, Johnson, Brett, and Jones, Ellis (2012) 'Lifestyle Movements: Exploring the Intersection of Lifestyle and Social Movements', *Social Movement Studies* 11(1): 1–20.

Hand Gesture Palm Card Descriptors (2011) (x6) Occupy Wall Street Archives Working Group Records, TAM 630, Box 4, Folder 11, 'Feb 2012', Notebook, Organizational Documents – Signs, 2011, New York, NY: Tamiment Library/ Robert F. Wagner Labor Archives, New York University.

Harcourt, Bernard E. (2013) 'Political Disobedience', in W. J. T. Mitchell, B. E. Harcourt, and M. Taussig *Occupy: Three Inquiries in Disobedience*, Chicago, IL and London: University of Chicago Press, pp. 45–92.

Helmore, Edward (2015) 'Collecting the Art of Protest at Brooklyn's Interference Archive', *Guardian*, October 15. Online at https://www.theguardian.com/ artanddesign/2015/oct/14/art-of-protest-interference-archive-brooklyn. Accessed February 21, 2018.

Hodder, Jake (2017) 'On Absence and Abundance: Biography as Method in Archival Research', *Area* 49(4): 452–59.

Holpuch, Amanda (2013) 'New York's Moma Acquires Occupy Wall Street Art Prints', *Guardian*, October 10. Online at https://www.theguardian.com/world/2013/ oct/10/moma-acquires-occupy-wall-street-art-prints. Accessed August 4, 2018.

Hooper-Greenhill, Eilean (1992) *Museums and the Shaping of Knowledge*, London and New York, NY: Routledge.

Hudgins, Sarita (2011a) 'Intro to Direct Democracy – Facilitation Training', Information by Craig Stephens – October 2011, Occupy Wall Street Archives Working Group Records, TAM 630, Box 1, Folder 2.18, Organizational Documents Occupy Wall Street 2011, New York, NY: Tamiment Library/Robert F. Wagner Labor Archives, New York University.

Hudgins, Sarita (2011b) 'Comment on Thread of November 13th Hardware Receipt for Finance', Discussion Post, Occupy Wall Street Archives Google Groups Forum, November 24. Online at https://groups.google.com/forum/#!topic/ows-archives/3g-1UxW_Yf0. Accessed August 8, 2018.

Humphries, Clare and Smith, Aaron C. T. (2014) 'Talking Objects: Towards a Post-Social Research Framework for Exploring Object Narratives', *Organization* 21(4): 477–94.

James, Paul (2013) 'Closing Reflections: Confronting Contradictions in Biographies of Nations and Persons', *Humanities Research* XIX(1): 121–37.

Jayadev, Arjun (2011) 'Reading the Signs at the Occupy Movement', *Economic and Political Weekly* 46(49): 28–31.

Jimerson, Randall C. (2013) 'Archivists and Social Responsibility: A Response to Mark Greene', *American Archivist* 76(2): 335–45.

Johnson, Timothy (2016) Email to Kylie Message, October 28.

Judkis, M. (2011) 'Occupy Wall Street Signs: Which Should Go in the Smithsonian?' *Washington Post*, October 24.

Keenan, Elizabeth K. and Darms, Lisa (2013) 'Safe Space: The Riot Grrrl Collection', *Archivaria* 76(Fall): 55–74.

Kessler-Harris, Alice (2009) 'Why Biography', *American Historical Review* 114(3): 625–30.

Kilkenny, Allison (2012) 'The Rush to Archive Occupy', *Nation*, January 2. Online at https://www.thenation.com/article/rush-archive-occupy/. Accessed August 4, 2018.

Klein, Naomi (2011) 'The Most Important Thing in the World', *Occupied Wall Street Journal* 1(2): n.p., October 8.

Kopytoff, Igor (1988) 'The Cultural Biography of Things: Commoditization as Process', in A. Appadurai (ed.) *The Social Life of Things: Commodities in Cultural Perspective*, Cambridge: Cambridge University Press, pp. 64–91.

Manski, Rebecca (2011) 'What Liberty Square Means: The Progress of Revolutions', *Occupied Wall Street Journal* 1(2): n.p., October 8.

Maréchal, Garance (2010) 'Autoethnography', in A. J. Mills, G. Durepos, and E. Wiebe (eds.) *Encyclopedia of Case Study Research* (Vol. 2), Thousand Oaks, CA: Sage Publications, pp. 43–45.

McGeachan, Cheryl, Forsyth, Isla, and Hasty, William (2012) 'Certain Subjects? Working with Biography and Life-Writing in Historical Geography', *Historical Geography* 40: 169–85.

McKee, Yates (2016) *Strike Art: Contemporary Art and the Post-Occupy Condition*, London and New York, NY: Verso Books.

McVeigh, Karen (2011) 'Occupy Wall Street's Women Struggle to Make Their Voices Heard'. *Guardian*, November 30. Online at https://www.theguardian.com/world/2011/nov/30/occupy-wall-street-women-voices. Accessed March 20, 2018.

'Meeting Minutes between Jan–Feb 2012' (n.d.) 'Intro to Direct Democracy – Facilitation Training', Information by Craig Stephens – October 2011, Occupy Wall Street Archives Working Group Records, TAM 630, Box 2, Organizational documents – Archives Working Group 2011–2013, New York, NY: Tamiment Library/Robert F. Wagner Labor Archives, New York University.

Mesle, Sarah (2017) '"'America' Is Not the Object": An Interview with Kandice Chuh, President of the American Studies Association', *Los Angeles Review of Books*, November 9. Online at https://lareviewofbooks.org/article/america-is-not-the-object-an-interview-with-kandice-chuh-president-of-the-american-studies-association/. Accessed February 21, 2018.

Message, Kylie (2014) *Museums and Social Activism: Engaged Protest*, London and New York, NY: Routledge.

Message, Kylie (2015) 'Contentious Politics and Museums as Contact Zones', in A. Witcomb and K. Message (eds.) *Museum Theory*, Chichester: Wiley Blackwell, pp. 253–82.

Message, Kylie (2017a) 'Occupy Collection/Grant', Email to Timothy Johnson, September 4.

Message, Kylie (2017b) 'Re: Introduction and Query', Email to Timothy Johnson, March 10.

Message, Kylie (2018a) *The Disobedient Museum: Writing at the Edge*, London and New York, NY: Routledge.

Message, Kylie (2018b) *Museums and Racism*, London and New York, NY: Routledge.

Miller, James (2018) 'What Does Democracy Look Like? On Occupy Wall Street, Protest Chants, And Participatory Democracy', *Literary Hub*, September 21. Online at https://lithub.com/what-does-democracy-look-like/. Accessed January 16, 2019.

'Minutes from Meeting with Tamiment' (August 3, n.y.) Occupy Wall Street Archives Working Group Records, TAM 630, Box 2, Organizational Documents – Archives Working Group 2011–2012, New York, NY: Tamiment Library/ Robert F. Wagner Labor Archives, New York University.

Mitchell, William J. T. (2012) 'Space, Revolution: The Arts of Occupation', *Critical Inquiry* 39(1): 8–32.

Mitchell, William J. T. (2013a) 'Preface', in W. J. T. Mitchell, B. E. Harcourt, and M. Taussig *Occupy: Three Inquiries in Disobedience*, Chicago, IL and London: University of Chicago Press, pp. vii–xv.

Mitchell, William J. T. (2013b) 'Image, Space, Revolution: The Arts of Occupation', in W. J. T. Mitchell, B. E. Harcourt, and M. Taussig *Occupy: Three Inquiries in Disobedience*, Chicago, IL and London: University of Chicago Press, pp. 93–130.

Molenda, James (2011a) 'Update on Seized Library Items', Discussion Post, Occupy Wall Street Archives Google Groups Forum, November 17. Online at https://groups. google.com/forum/#!topic/ows-archives/Aj4QGA-eSwU. Accessed August 8, 2018.

Molenda, James (2011b) 'RE: Budget Fail', Discussion Post, Occupy Wall Street Archives Google Groups Forum. Online at https://groups.google.com/ forum/#!topic/ows-archives/_UOTAyRjM40. Accessed August 8, 2018.

Moloney, Kevin (2005) 'Trust and Public Relations: Center and Edge', *Public Relations Review* 31: 550–55.

Monk, Ray (2007) 'Life without Theory: Biography as an Exemplar of Philosophical Understanding', *Poetics Today* 28(3): 527–71.

Ng, Yvonne (2011) 'RE: Budget Fail', Occupy Wall Street Archives Google Groups Forum, November 13. Online at https://groups.google.com/forum/#!topic/ows-archives/_UOTAyRjM40. Accessed August 8, 2018.

Ng, Yvonne (2012a) 'Public Forum on OWS Archives on February 5th', *Activist Archivists*, February 2. Online at http://activist-archivists.org/wp/?p=445. Accessed August 4, 2018.

Ng, Yvonne (2012b) 'OWS Archives Share Day, March 31 2012', *Activist Archivists*, March 23. Online at http://activist-archivists.org/wp/?p=706. Accessed August 4, 2018.

'NY Archives Week Symposium Program' (n.d.) Occupy Wall Street Archives Working Group Records, TAM 630, Box 2, Folder 2.9, Organizational Documents – Archives Working Group 2011–2012, New York, NY: Tamiment Library/Robert F. Wagner Labor Archives, New York University.

Occupied Wall Street Journal (2011) 'Editorial Note: No List of Demands', *Occupied Wall Street Journal* 1(2): n.p., October 8.

Ott, Julia (2016) 'Occupied Wall Street Journal: Object Essay', *Stories: Movements and Causes*, Museum of the City of New York, November 7. Online at https:// www.mcny.org/story/occupied-wall-street-journal. Accessed August 4, 2018.

Ough, Tom (2015) 'Anonymous: How the Guy Fawkes Mask Became an Icon of the Protest Movement', *Independent*, November 4. Online at https://www.independent. co.uk/news/uk/home-news/anonymous-how-the-guy-fawkes-mask-became-an-icon-of-the-protest-movement-a6720831.html. Accessed August 4, 2018.

'OWS Archives Budget Proposal' Revised as of January 13, 2012 (2012) Occupy Wall Street Archives Working Group Records, TAM 630, Box 2, Folder 2.4, Organizational Documents – Archives Working Group 2012, New York, NY: Tamiment Library/Robert F. Wagner Labor Archives, New York University.

OWS Structure Working Group (n.d.) 'OWS Structure Proposal', Occupy Wall Street Archives Working Group Records, TAM 630, Box 2, Folder 2.14, Organizational Documents – Archives Working Group 2011, New York, NY: Tamiment Library/Robert F. Wagner Labor Archives, New York University.

Parry, Ken and Boyle, Maree (2009) 'Organizational Autoethnography', in D. A. Buchanan and A. Bryman (eds.) *The SAGE Handbook of Organizational Research Methods*, London: SAGE, pp. 690–702.

Pearce, Susan (1992) *Museums, Objects and Collections*, Washington, DC: Smithsonian Institution Press.

Pearce, Susan M. (1994) 'Objects as Meaning: Or Narrating the Past', in S. M. Pearce (ed.) *Interpreting Objects and Collections*, London: Routledge, pp. 19–29.

Pearce, Susan M. (1998) *Collecting in Contemporary Practice*, London: Sage.

Pearce, Susan M. (2010) 'Foreword', in S. H. Dudley (ed.) *Museum Materialities: Objects, Engagements, Interpretations*, London: Routledge, pp. xiv–xix.

Perricci, Anna (2012) 'NY Times Coverage', Discussion Post, Occupy Wall Street Archives Google Groups Forum, May 3. Online at https://groups.google.com/forum/#!topic/ows-archives/W6_rgo1wWZQ. Accessed August 8, 2018.

Questionnaire (n.d.) Occupy Wall Street Archives Working Group Records, TAM 630, Box 2, Folder 2.10, Organizational Documents – Archives Working Group 2011–2012, New York, NY: Tamiment Library/Robert F. Wagner Labor Archives, New York University.

Reed-Danahay, Deborah (2011) 'Autobiography, Intimacy and Ethnography', in P. Atkinson, A. Coffey, S. Delamont, J. Lofland, and L. Lofland (eds.) *Handbook of Ethnography*, Sage, pp. 401–25. Online at http://dx.doi.org.virtual.anu.edu.au/10.4135/9781848608337. Accessed January 14, 2019.

Reich, Robert (2019) 'Trump is Using the Government as a Bargaining Chip – Like a Dictator Would', *Guardian*, January 11. Online at https://www.theguardian.com/commentisfree/2019/jan/10/trump-government-shutdown-democracy-power-dictatorship. Accessed January 14.

Reinecke, Juliane (2018) 'Social Movements and Prefigurative Organizing: Confronting Entrenched Inequalities in Occupy London', *Organization Studies* 39(9): 1299–321.

Riley, Dennis Roman (2012) '[DRAFT] Event Announcement: Who Will Keep the Archives of Occupy Wall Street?' Discussion Post and Attachment, Occupy Wall Street Archives Google Groups Forum, July 28. Online at https://groups.google.com/forum/#!topic/ows-archives/PQrXpYrzKQE. Accessed August 8, 2018.

Roberts, Amy (2011a) 'Occupy Wall Street Archive Mission Statement.docx', Discussion Post (and Attachment), Occupy Wall Street Archives Google Groups, December 1. Online at https://groups.google.com/forum/#!topic/ows-archives/V8iofbpsQPo. Accessed August 8, 2018.

Roberts, Amy (2011b) 'Raid on Tuesday Morning', Discussion Post, Occupy Wall Street Archives Google Groups, November 17. Online at https://groups.google.com/forum/#!topic/ows-archives/F4jxN8hD36c. Accessed August 8, 2018.

Roberts, Amy (2011c) 'Budget Fail', Discussion Post, Occupy Wall Street Archives Google Groups, November 12. Online at https://groups.google.com/forum/#!topic/ows-archives/_UOTAyRjM40. Accessed August 8, 2018.

Roberts, Amy (2011d) 'Spokescouncil', Discussion Post, Occupy Wall Street Archives Google Groups, November 11. Online at https://groups.google.com/forum/#!topic/ows-archives/sDSy_C6dso4. Accessed August 8, 2018.

Roberts, Amy (2011e) 'Fwd: Spokes Council Address and Documents', Discussion Post (and Attachment), Occupy Wall Street Archives Google Groups, November 8. Online at https://groups.google.com/forum/#!topic/ows-archives/_F02nGKeU1s. Accessed August 8, 2018.

Roberts, Amy (2017) 'Re: Shared Dropbox Folders', Email to Kylie Message, July 24 2017.

Roberts, Amy (n.d.a) Notebook, Occupy Wall Street Archives Working Group Records, TAM 630, Box 3, Folder 2.15, Organizational Documents – Archives Working Group 2011–2012, New York, NY: Tamiment Library/Robert F. Wagner Labor Archives, New York University.

Roberts, Amy (n.d.b) Notes, Occupy Wall Street Archives Working Group Records, TAM 630, Box 2, Folder 2.10, Organizational Documents – Archives Working Group 2011–2012, New York, NY: Tamiment Library/Robert F. Wagner Labor Archives, New York University.

Roberts, Amy (n.d.c) Notes, Occupy Wall Street Archives Working Group Records, TAM 630, Box 2, Folder 2.9, Organizational Documents – Archives Working Group 2011–2012, New York, NY: Tamiment Library/Robert F. Wagner Labor Archives, New York University.

Roberts, Amy (n.d.d) Notebook, Occupy Wall Street Archives Working Group Records, TAM 630, Box 2, Folder 2.7, Organizational Documents – Archives Working Group 2012, New York, NY: Tamiment Library/Robert F. Wagner Labor Archives, New York University.

Roberts, Amy (n.d.e) Notes in Feb 2012- Notebook, Occupy Wall Street Archives Working Group Records, TAM 630, Box 2, Folder 2.4, Organizational Documents – Archives Working Group 2011–2012, New York, NY: Tamiment Library/Robert F. Wagner Labor Archives, New York University.

Roberts, Amy (n.d.f) Notes, Occupy Wall Street Archives Working Group Records, TAM 630, Box 2, Folder 2.3, Organizational Documents – Archives Working Group 2011–2012, New York, NY: Tamiment Library/Robert F. Wagner Labor Archives, New York University.

Roberts, Amy (n.d.g) Notes, Occupy Wall Street Archives Working Group Records, TAM 630, Box 2, Folder 2.2, Organizational Documents – Archives Working Group 2011–2012, New York, NY: Tamiment Library/Robert F. Wagner Labor Archives, New York University.

Roberts, Amy (n.d.h) Transcripts of Unpublished Interviews with Members of the Archives Working Group, Occupy Wall Street Archives Working Group Records,

TAM 630, Box 2, Folder 2.2, Organizational Documents – Archives Working Group 2011–2012, New York, NY: Tamiment Library/Robert F. Wagner Labor Archives, New York University.

Roberts, Amy (n.d.i) Typed Paper, Occupy Wall Street Archives Working Group Records, TAM 630, Box 2, Folder 2.8, Organizational Documents – Archives Working Group 2012, New York, NY: Tamiment Library/Robert F. Wagner Labor Archives, New York University.

Roberts, Amy (n.d.j) Minutes from Meeting with Tamiment, August 3, Occupy Wall Street Archives Working Group Records, TAM 630, Box 2, Folder 2.8, Organizational Documents – Archives Working Group 2012, New York, NY: Tamiment Library/Robert F. Wagner Labor Archives, New York University.

Roberts, Amy (n.d.k) Meeting Minutes between Jan–Feb 2012, Occupy Wall Street Archives Working Group Records, TAM 630, Box 2, Folder 2.6, Organizational Documents – Archives Working Group 2011–2013, New York, NY: Tamiment Library/Robert F. Wagner Labor Archives, New York University.

Roberts, Amy (n.d.l) Notes in From Sept 17 to Nov 7 2011 Notebook, Occupy Wall Street Archives Working Group Records, TAM 630, Box 2, Folder 2.5, Organizational Documents – Archives Working Group 2011, New York, NY: Tamiment Library/Robert F. Wagner Labor Archives, New York University.

Sacks, Jennifer (2011) 'Occupy Your Mind: The People's Library', *Occupied Wall Street Journal* 3: n.p., October 22.

Salazar, Cristian and Herschaft, Randy (2011) 'Occupy Wall Street: Major Museums and Organizations Collect Materials Produced by Occupy Movement', *Huffington Post*, November 24. Online at http://www.huffingtonpost.com/2011/12/24/occupy-wall-street-museums-organizations_n_1168893.html. Accessed August 4, 2018.

Samtani, Hiten (2011) 'The Anarchivists: Who Owns the Occupy Wall Street Narrative?' *Brooklyn Ink*, December 26. Online at http://brooklynink. org/2011/12/26/39230-the-anarchivists-who-owns-the-occupy-wall-street-narrative/. Accessed February 21, 2018.

Schneider, Nathan (2011) 'No Leaders, No Violence: What Diversity of Tactics Means for Occupy Wall Street', in S. van Gelder (ed.) *This Changes Everything: Occupy Wall Street and the 99% Movement*, San Francisco, CA: Berrett-Koehler Publishers, Inc., pp. 39–44.

Schneider, Nathan (2013a) 'Occupy, After Occupy', *Nation*, September 5. Online at https://www.thenation.com/article/occupy-after-occupy/. Accessed February 21, 2018.

Schneider, Nathan (2013b) *Thank You, Anarchy: Notes from the Occupy Apocalypse*, Berkeley and Los Angeles, CA: University of California Press.

Schneider, Nathan (n.d.) 'Occupation for Dummies. How It Came About, What It Means, How It Works, and Everything', *Occupied Wall Street Journal* 1: n.p.

Schuessler, Jennifer (2012a) 'Academia Occupied by Occupy', *New York Times*, April 30. Online at https://www.nytimes.com/2012/05/01/books/academia-becomes-occupied-with-occupy-movement.html. Accessed August 4, 2018.

Schuessler, Jennifer (2012b) 'Occupy Wall Street: From the Streets to the Archives', *ArtsBeat: New York Times Blog*, May 3. Online at http://artsbeat.blogs.nytimes.

com/2012/05/02/occupy-wall-street-from-the-streets-to-the-archives. Accessed August 4, 2018.

Schwartz, Joan M. and Cook, Terry (2002) 'Archives, Records and Power: The Making of Modern Memory', *Archival Science* 2(1–2): 1–19.

Sellie, Alycia, Goldstein, Jesse, Fair, Molly, and Hoyer, Jennifer (2015) 'Interference Archive: A Free Space for Social Movement Culture', *Archival Science* 15: 453–72.

Smith, Samara (2011) 'Proposal to Deposit Restricted Access Oral Histories with Tamiment Attachment to Proposal to Deed Some Oral Histories to Tamiment', Discussion Post, Occupy Wall Street Archives Google Groups Forum, November 14. Online at https://groups.google.com/forum/#!topic/ows-archives/ ID8KxU70aGg. Accessed August 8, 2018.

Smithsonian National Museum of American History Kenneth E. Behring Center (2017) 'Statement Regarding Collecting Political History' (Press Release), January 23. Online at http://americanhistory.si.edu/press/releases/statement-political-history. Accessed January 14, 2019.

Snow, David A. (2004) 'Social Movements as Challenges to Authority: Resistance to an Emerging Conceptual Hegemony', *Research in Social Movements, Conflicts and Change* 25: 3–25.

Solnit, Rebecca (2011) 'The Occupation of Hope: Letter to a Dead Man', in S. van Gelder (ed.) *This Changes Everything: Occupy Wall Street and the 99% Movement*, San Francisco, CA: Berrett-Koehler Publishers, Inc., pp. 77–82.

Star, Susan Leigh (1999) 'The Ethnography of Infrastructure', *American Behavioral Scientist* 43(3): 377–91.

Stoler, Ann Laura (2002) 'Colonial Archives and the Arts of Governance', *Archival Science* 2(1–2): 87–109.

Stoler, Ann Laura (2010) *Along the Archival Grain: Epistemic Anxieties and Colonial Common Sense*, Princeton, NJ: Princeton University Press.

Sulehka (2011) 'RE: Budget Fail', Discussion Post, Occupy Wall Street Archives Google Groups Forum, November 13. Online at https://groups.google.com/ forum/#!topic/ows-archives/_UOTAyRjM40. Accessed August 8, 2018.

Tamiment Library and Robert F. Wagner Labor Archive (2014) Guide to the Paul Hammacott Occupy Wall Street Screen Prints Collection TAM.641, May 22, New York, NY: Tamiment Library and Robert F. Wagner Labor Archive. Online at http://dlib.nyu.edu/findingaids/html/tamwag/tam_641/tam_641.html. Accessed June 21, 2018.

Tamiment Library and Robert F. Wagner Labor Archive (2018) Guide to the Occupy Wall Street Archives Working Group Records TAM.630, January 10, New York, NY: Tamiment Library and Robert F. Wagner Labor Archive. Online at http:// dlib.nyu.edu/findingaids/html/tamwag/tam_630/tam_630.html. Accessed June 21, 2018.

Taussig, Michael (2013) 'I'm so Angry I Made a Sign', in W. J. T. Mitchell, B. E. Harcourt, and M. Taussig *Occupy: Three Inquiries in Disobedience*, Chicago, IL and London: University of Chicago Press, pp. 3–44.

Taylor, Jaime and Loeb, Zachary (2014) 'Librarian is My Occupation: A History of the People's Library of Occupy Wall Street', in M. Morrone (ed.) *Informed*

Agitation: Library and Information Skills in Social Justice Movements and Beyond, Sacramento, CA: Library Juice Press, pp. 271–88.

Third, Amanda (2016) 'The Tactical Researcher: Cultural Studies Research as Pedagogy', in A. Hickey (ed.) *The Pedagogies of Cultural Studies*, New York, NY and London: Routledge, pp. 93–115.

Tilley, Christopher (2011) 'Ethnography and Material Culture', in P. Atkinson, A. Coffey, S. Delamont, J. Lofland, and L. Lofland (eds.) *Handbook of Ethnography*, London: Sage, pp. 258–72. Online at http://dx.doi.org.virtual.anu.edu.au/10.4135/9781848608337. Accessed January 14, 2019.

Tisdale, Rainey (2011) 'Do History Museums Still Need Objects?' *History News* June(Summer): 19–24. Online at http://aaslhcommunity.org/historynews/files/2011/08/RaineySmr11Links.pdf. Accessed March 25, 2019.

Weber, Klaus and King, Brayden (2014) 'Social Movement Theory and Organization Studies', in P. Adler, P. Du Gay, and G. Morgan (eds.) *Sociology, Social Theory, and Organization Studies: Contemporary Currents*, Oxford: Oxford University Press, pp. 487–509.

White, Micah (2016) *The End of Protest: A New Playbook for Revolution*, Toronto: Alfred A. Knopf Canada.

Wilkening, Susie (2009) 'Community Engagement and Objects – Mutually Exclusive?' *Museum Audience Insight*, July 27. Online at http://reachadvisors.typepad.com/museum_audience_insight/2009/07/community-engagement-and-objects-mutually-exclusive.html. Link no longer live.

Wilkening, Susie and Donnis, Erica (2008) 'Authenticity? It Means Everything', *History News* 63(4, Autumn): 18–23.

Yanow, Dvora, Ybema, Sierk, and Van Hulst, Merlijn (2012) 'Practising Organizational Ethnography', in G. Symon and C. Cassell (eds.) *The Practice of Qualitative Organizational Research: Core Methods and Current Challenges*, London: Sage, pp. 331–50.

Ybema, Sierk, Yanow, Dvora, Wels, Harry, and Kamsteeg, Frans H. (2009) 'Studying Everyday Organizational Life', in S. Ybema, D. Yanow, F. H. Kamsteeg, and H. Wels (eds.) *Organizational Ethnography: Studying the Complexity of Everyday Life*, London: Sage, pp. 1–20.

Young, Jeffrey R. (2012) '"Occupy" Movement Presents New Challenges', *Chronicle of Higher Education*, April 3. Online at http://chronicle.com/blogs/wiredcampus/for-archivists-%E2%80%98occupy%E2%80%99-movement-presents-new-challenges/35929. Accessed August 4, 2018.

Zilber, Tammar B. (2014) 'Beyond a Single Organization: Challenges and Opportunities in Doing Field Level Ethnography', *Journal of Organizational Ethnography* 3(1): 96–113.

#jez3Prez & Atchu (2012) 'On the Question of the Anarchives of Occupy Wall Street', *emisférica (Journal of the Hemispheric Institute of Performance and Politics)* 9(1–2, Summer). Online at http://hemisphericinstitute.org/hemi/en/e-misferica-91/jez3prezaatchu. Accessed February 21, 2018.

Index

For Product Safety Concerns and Information please contact our EU
representative GPSR@taylorandfrancis.com
Taylor & Francis Verlag GmbH, Kaufingerstraße 24, 80331 München, Germany

www.ingramcontent.com/pod-product-compliance
Lightning Source LLC
Chambersburg PA
CBHW061329220326
41599CB00026B/5097